Jesus—Death Destroyer

Group

Loveland, Colorado

www.group.com

Group resources actually work!

This Group resource helps you focus on **"The 1 Thing™"**— a life-changing relationship with Jesus Christ. "The 1 Thing" incorporates our **R.E.A.L.** approach to ministry. It reinforces a growing friendship with Jesus, encourages long-term learning, and results in life transformation, because it's:

Relational
Learner-to-learner interaction enhances learning and builds Christian friendships.

Experiential
What learners experience through discussion and action sticks with them up to 9 times longer than what they simply hear or read.

Applicable
The aim of Christian education is to equip learners to be both hearers and doers of God's Word.

Learner-based
Learners understand and retain more when the learning process takes into consideration how they learn best.

BibleVenture Centers™: Jesus—Death Destroyer
Copyright © 2005 Group Publishing, Inc.

Visit our Web site: **www.group.com**

Credits
Author: Jody Brolsma
Creative Development Editor: Mikal Keefer
Chief Creative Officer: Joani Schultz
Copy Editor: Ann M. Diaz
Art Director/Designer: Helen H. Harrison
Illustrator: Matt Wood
Cover Art Director/Designer: Bambi Eitel
Cover Illustrator: Patty O'Friel
Production Manager: Peggy Naylor

Unless otherwise noted, Scripture taken from the HOLY BIBLE, NEW INTERNATIONAL VERSION®. Copyright © 1973, 1978, 1984 by International Bible Society. Used by permission of Zondervan Publishing House. All rights reserved.

Library of Congress Cataloging-in-Publication Data
Jesus, death destroyer.-- 1st American pbk.
    p. cm. -- (BibleVenture centers)
  ISBN 0-7644-2793-8 (pbk. : alk. paper)
  1. Jesus Christ--Biography--Passion Week--Study and teaching. 2. Bible. N.T. Gospels--Study and teaching. 3. Christian education of children. I. Group Publishing. II. Series.

  BT431.3.J47 2004
  268'.432--dc22

                        2004018865

10 9 8 7 6 5 4 3 2 1   14 13 12 11 10 09 08 07 06 05

Printed in the United States of America.

Contents

Welcome to Bible Ventures™

Ever wish you could connect with *all* your kids, not just the few who seem to naturally enjoy your classroom?

Most Christian educators find themselves wondering why Nancy tracks along with the lesson while Jason is busy poking his neighbors. And why does Darrell light up when it's time to be in a drama, but he'd rather eat worms than do a craft project?

If you've wondered if you're a poor teacher or you have a roomful of aliens, relax. You're dealing with learning styles—and covering all the bases is a challenge every classroom leader faces. You're not alone.

God wired different children (and adults!) differently. That's a good thing—otherwise, we'd live in a world populated solely by mechanical engineers. Or maybe everyone would be an artist and our world would be a dazzling burst of color and music—but the bridges would all fall down.

We *need* to have different people in the world...and in the church.

BibleVentures gives you the opportunity for hands-on exploration of key Bible events using a variety of learning styles. You'll open up the truth of the Bible Point and the Scripture passage to a wide variety of children, whether they learn best through their ears, their fingers, or their eyes. You'll engage children and provide a "wow!" of surprise as kids move from one BibleVenture Center to another.

And best of all, you'll know that you're helping long-term, high-impact learning to happen. Your kids won't just *hear* God's Word; they'll *experience* it. You'll plant it deep in their hearts and minds.

So get ready for a learning adventure. *You'll* know you're providing a balanced, learning experience that taps a range of learning styles, but your kids won't know...or care.

They'll just know they're having a blast learning—and that, in your class, you speak their language.

How to Use This Program

Each week children will gather as one large group at **The Depot**—the launching spot for their weekly adventures. Here they'll experience a fun opening that draws their attention to the Bible Point.

From The Depot, children move with their designated teams to one of the four **Venture Centers.** Children will remain in their Venture Centers for forty minutes and, while there, dive deep into one portion of the Bible story through dramas, games, music, puppets, or other fun activities. Then everyone returns to The Depot for a time of closing and celebration.

Included in your BibleVentures *book are:*
- 1 leader's section,
- 1 set of leader job descriptions,
- 4 Venture Center Leaders sections,
- 4 reproducible visa sheets, and
- 1 reproducible CD.

You'll use these resources to lead children on an exciting and interactive four-week journey through the life of Jesus!

Also included for your use, should you choose to use them, are
- a sample invitation letter to help you encourage kids in your church and your neighborhood to attend,
- BibleVenture Center Leader encouragers—so your volunteers grow in their commitment in serving kids and Christ,
- a brief article to send to your leaders about how to connect with kids, and
- a teacher training session!

Ready to get started? Here's how...

1. Recruit leaders.
You'll need five Venture Center Leaders for this BibleVenture.

One leader will oversee The Depot gatherings. The other four leaders will run the four Venture Centers. Review the different Venture Centers *before* recruiting leaders; that way you'll be able to match up the major learning style used in each center with someone who enjoys connecting with kids in that way.

Bible Point Alert!

As children move through this BibleVenture program, they'll discover a foundational Bible truth—a Bible Point. The Bible Point is mentioned often in each Venture Center. Encourage your kids to explore the Bible Point, and live it out every day of the week!

For instance, if you have a center that uses lots of music, find a bouncy, fun song leader who loves Jesus and loves kids. If a center uses art to tell a Bible story, ask an artistic, crafty person to lead that center.

One plus of the BibleVenture method of teaching is that teachers get to use their strengths! But that only happens if you're careful to match needs of the centers with the gifts of the teachers.

The person leading The Depot will have new material to present each week, while the Venture Center Leaders will teach one session four times over the course of four weeks. Since a new group of children rotates through the center each week, the leader can use the same lesson four times!

This approach allows for less weekly preparation on the part of your center leaders. And they'll improve from week to week as they fine-tune their presentations.

You'll also need some BibleVenture Buddies.

These are adults or capable teenagers who each befriend a small group of children. We call those small groups "Venture Teams." BibleVenture Buddies hang out with their Venture Teams and serve as a guide, facilitator, and friend.

BibleVenture Buddies don't prepare a lesson or teach. Instead, they get to know their kids. Buddies learn names, pray for the children on their Venture Teams, and reach out to kids in appropriate ways. If Jodie is absent, it's the BibleVenture Buddy who sends a postcard to let her know she was missed. If Jodie is sick, it's her BibleVenture Buddy who calls to encourage her.

BibleVenture Buddies show up for class ten minutes early so they're ready to greet children. They travel with kids to different centers each week and enthusiastically join in to play the games, do the crafts, sing the music, and do whatever else the children do.

Your BibleVenture Buddies aren't teachers, but they help kids connect with the Bible truth being taught in each center. Because they get to know their kids, they're perfectly positioned to help relate the Bible truths to individual kids' lives.

How many BibleVenture Buddies will you need? It depends on how many children participate in your program. For purposes of crowd control and relationship-building, it's best if Venture Teams consist of between five and seven children, and you'll need one BibleVenture Buddy for each team. You'll keep the same team of children together throughout your four-week adventure.

And here's a tip for leaders: Look for BibleVenture Buddies among people who *haven't* been Christian education volunteers in the past. Clearly communicate that you're not asking these folks to teach; you're asking them

to be a friend to a small group of children. This job is completely *different* from being a Sunday school teacher!

2. Give each leader his or her section of this book.

Don't worry—those sections are reproducible for use in your local church. So is the CD, so ask a teenager in your congregation to burn a copy for each of the leaders. Copying CDs is easy, inexpensive, and—so long as you use the CDs in your church only—completely legal!

Here's how to distribute the pages:
- The Depot: pages 25–41
- Venture Center One: The Games Center: pages 43–49
- Venture Center Two: The Storytelling Center: pages 51–56
- Venture Center Three: The Art Center: pages 57–63
- Venture Center Four: The Drama Center: pages 65–76

3. Create groups of children.

When you're creating individual Venture Teams, form your teams with children of various ages. This allows older children to help the younger ones and to be role models. It also results in fewer discipline problems.

"What?" you may be thinking. "Not keep all my third-grade girls together? They'll go on strike!"

Trust us: When you create Venture Teams that combine several ages, *especially* if you have an adult volunteer travel with each team, you'll see fewer discipline issues arise. Children may groan a bit at first, but reassure them that they'll be able to hang out with their same-age buddies before the BibleVenture starts.

Besides, when you use mixed-age groupings, you're *also* separating your fifth-grade boys!

Some churches choose to create multi-age groups by combining first-through third-graders and then creating separate groups of fourth- and fifth-graders. This is also an option.

Help children remember what Venture Teams they're in by assigning each team a color. Or get into the theme of this BibleVenture and ask Venture Teams to come up with theme-based names for themselves!

As you assign children to their Venture Teams, make a notation on their name tags and on their BibleVenture Visas as to which team they're on. That way when kids sign in each week at The Depot ticket window, they'll quickly remember what team to join for the remainder of the program.

Be certain each child and adult has a name tag to wear each week. Name tags allow everyone to know each other's names (instead of saying, "You, in the blue shirt"), *and* they allow leaders to know that a child has signed in. You can make permanent name tags that kids and leaders reuse each week or write names on self-stick labels. A quick and easy way for kids to know what teams they're on is to use name tags in colors that correspond to their Venture Teams. Or use white labels and write names in colorful ink that corresponds to Venture Teams.

Please note: Because you have four Venture Centers going at the same time, you need to form four groupings of children to attend them. If you have four Venture Teams, it's easy—just send one team to each Venture Center. If you have more than that, do what you can to have an approximately even number of kids (or teams) in each of the centers. It makes life easier for center leaders if they see about the same number of kids each week.

If you have a smaller number of children—fewer than fifteen—participating in your program, you might consider keeping all the kids together and doing a different Venture Center each week.

4. Make copies of visas.

You'll want a visa for each child in attendance, plus extras for visitors. Visas are distributed the first time you meet, so make copies now and get that task out of the way.

It's perfectly legal for you to make as many copies as you need for your local church use.

5. Walk through the entire BibleVenture with your volunteers.

Invite your leaders to sit down with you and talk through what they'll be doing, when they'll do it, and where they'll be serving. Many leaders like to know where they'll hold their class so they can think through the logistics of how to stage a drama or where to store supplies from week to week.

Besides, you'll want to pray with your team and thank them for loving kids and helping kids discover Bible truths. A quick meeting is one good way to do that.

That's it—five easy steps to memorable, exciting, fun learning! *BibleVentures* is easy—and it's a blast!

During this four-week adventure about Jesus' death and resurrection, children will learn 1 John 4:11, which says, "Dear friends, since God so loved us, we also ought to love one another." Kids will discover relevant, practical ways they can share God's powerful love with those around them. Children will learn and apply this verse through activities in The Depot and in the Venture Centers. Consider creating a poster, banner, or other visual with the Venture Verse on it to display during this BibleVenture.

It's important to note that what you're after isn't just that kids can recite the verse—that wouldn't take more than ten minutes and a stack of candy bar rewards.

What you want is for children to plant the truth of the words deep in their hearts and minds. You want kids to make the connection that God loves them; Jesus' death and resurrection prove God's love.

And because God loves us, we can share his love with others. What fun!

At BibleVentures you won't have children memorize a blizzard of Scripture passages that will be tucked in their short-term memory today and totally gone tomorrow. Instead, kids will be exposed to the meaning of the words and the impact of the truth of God's knowing them, loving them, and wanting to change their lives and help them change their worlds.

If you choose to make Bible memory a larger part of your BibleVenture Center program, great. It's easy to integrate more verses into the program. But remember that when it comes to bringing about true life change, "less is more." It's far better to focus on one verse that sinks deep into how children view themselves before God than to slide a bunch of words into their heads.

The Venture Visas

Make one BibleVenture Visa for each child. Photocopy the BibleVenture Visas on pages 15–19. Place the cover on top and the pages inside in any order—the order isn't important as children can quickly find the appropriate page when asked to do so. And have a visa for each child—kids *love* having their own special visas!

Make it easier for kids to know what teams they're on by having the color of the construction paper for each team be unique and consistent.

Each week children will have their BibleVenture Visas stamped, stickered, or signed by a leader. In this BibleVenture program, that happens at The Depot, in the opening or closing program.

At the closing, BibleVenture Buddies will gather the visas and return them to the leader of The Depot, who'll keep the visas for the following week.

At the last closing, children will receive them to take home.

This visa is the property of

_____

and secures safe transport and assures the bearer admittance to each Venture Center.

The Travel Plan

Use the following chart to help you plan where children will travel each week.

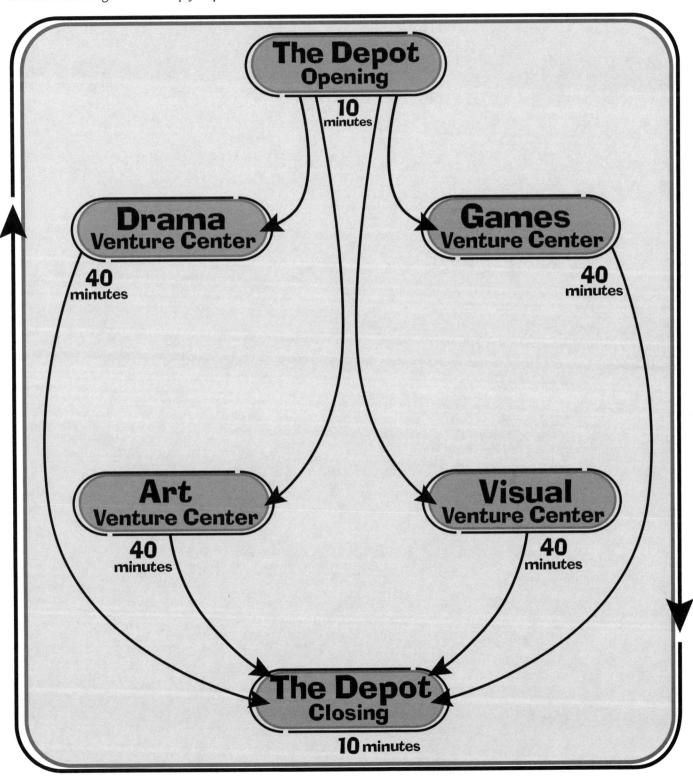

Make the Most of Your BibleVenture

For the next four weeks you'll be exploring the last days of Christ's ministry on earth, so make the most of it and have fun with décor and costumes. You can keep it simple with a few posters, or go all out and create an entire Jerusalem landscape. Picture your leaders wearing costumes, and think what you could accomplish if you recruited a crew with scissors and thread to make simple costumes for all the kids to wear!

Here are some ideas:

Costumes for dramas

The basis for most costumes is a tunic. For an easy-make, quick-wear tunic, fold a length of fabric in half and cut a half-circle from the fold to make an opening for the head. Use a piece of rope or thin length of fabric as a belt. It's quick and pulls on over clothing easily.

For accessories, shop first at thrift stores or second-hand shops. You can buy inexpensive costume jewelry, props, and clothing you can easily adapt. Keep in mind that for the purposes of your dramas, you need only one definitive prop to establish a character. For instance, while you can put a costume on the Jesus character, you need only wrap a towel around the waist of the child playing Jesus for the story of the foot washing, and that will remind everyone who's playing the part of Jesus. Don't fear *simple* costuming: a robe, a collar, or a piece of purple cloth wrapped around shoulders. Simple isn't bad! The costuming suggestions below assume you have time and resources to turn your dramas into mini-productions.

● Angels

Begin with white tunics. Cut wings from white cardboard and strap them to the back. If you have the time and budget, add halos made from gold tinsel and harps. Finish the costume with white wigs and dramatic white makeup.

● Mary

Use burlap to make your tunic. Go barefoot. Scruff up your hair, and smudge your face with a dark eyebrow pencil.

● Jesus

Add a white sash around the middle of a solid-colored bathrobe. Wear a dark beard and leather (or brown plastic) sandals.

● *Disciples*

Wear bathrobes of various colors. Add sandals or go barefoot.

Scenery

Consider giving your four sessions an extra bit of fun by creating a set in the room where you'll have The Depot segments of your program. You could turn a stage or room into a Jerusalem marketplace, the inside of a Bible-times home, or the hilltop where Jesus was crucified.

If you keep the set general in nature—an outdoor Bible-times set—then you can probably use it for your dramas, too.

You can create a set by...

● painting on large sheets of paper to make backdrops, then hanging them on the walls.

● setting up canopies to create shops. Drape colorful cloth over the top of the canopy, then "dress" the shops with tables displaying pottery or baskets filled with produce.

● placing a low table (like a coffee table) in the middle of your Bible-times home setting. Set large pillows on the floor around the table, and set out bread and fresh fruit for the inhabitants to enjoy.

● drawing palm trees or olive trees on sheets of cardboard, and taping them to the walls.

● attaching twinkling Christmas lights to the ceiling if you'd like to approximate a night scene.

The Depot

For the next four weeks, you'll lead The Depot portion of the BibleVentures program. Each week children will gather at The Depot for an opening time and a closing time. Each segment lasts about ten minutes.

At The Depot, kids sing, review the Venture Verse, and participate in an attention-grabbing experience that introduces the Bible Point. The following lessons will provide all the information you need to have a great time leading this segment of the BibleVenture program!

After the opening, groups of children (Venture Teams) will travel to Venture Centers. Children will stay in the Venture Centers for forty minutes, then return to The Depot for a time of closing and celebration.

During this BibleVenture, children will explore Jesus' death and resurrection. Children will discover that God loves us, and they'll determine new ways to show their love for God. That's an important lesson to learn...and put into action!

You'll see the "God loves us" Bible Point mentioned several times in your lessons. That's intentional: Repetition helps children hear and remember. And by the end of this BibleVenture program, children will have considered the many ways they can demonstrate God's love, and they'll develop a closer relationship with a loving heavenly Father.

You've been carefully selected to serve in this role. You have the abilities, attitude, and love of Jesus and kids that it takes to engage and involve children. You'll make good use of those abilities in this program!

Here's a quick outline of your responsibilities as leader of The Depot:

1. Meet and greet kids.

You're the upfront face kids will see each week; it matters how you go out of your way to individually greet as many children as possible. A smile and handshake or pat on the back from you can make a child's day.

Because you'll be making the first impression, it's important you arrive *before* children come. You'll also need to set up and either supervise—or do—the distribution of visas.

2. Oversee visa distribution.

As children arrive at The Depot, they'll stop at the Depot ticket window to sign in, get their name tags, and pick up their BibleVenture Visas. The ticket window can be as simple as a table with a sign on it or as elaborate as a booth with a ticket window cut in it.

For an inexpensive, portable booth, set a refrigerator box on end and cut a door in the back and a ticket window in the front. Prime and paint the booth with bright colors, and you'll have a lightweight booth with room inside for one medium-size adult.

And while you should oversee this function, it's going to be very difficult for you to staff it and take care of everything else that's happening as you lead the program. There will always be children who come a little late and want to sign in while you're up front leading a song.

So unless you can be two places at once, it's important that you recruit a helper. We call that person the "Servant Leader" because he or she serves you and others—and that's true leadership!

You'll find a job description for the role of Servant Leader on page 83.

3. Set up for the opening and closing!

The following lessons will tell you everything you need to know. And though the required supplies are simple and easy to find, it will help if you plan ahead.

Again, your life will be far easier if you recruit a Servant Leader to keep the supply cabinet stocked and the sign-in and sign-out processes organized.

The Depot

God Loves Us

Venture Verse: "Dear friends, since God so loved us, we also ought to love one another" (1 John 4:11).

Supplies for Week 1
- large box filled with enough mini-sized candy bars for each child to have one
- gift wrap
- sheet of paper for gift tag
- CD player
- *BibleVentures: Jesus* CD

The Depot: *Opening*

Before the session, place the candy bars into smaller bags. Each bag should contain enough candy for one Venture Team. (This will make it easier to distribute the candy.) Place the bags inside a large box (the bigger the better), and gift-wrap the box.

The goal of this activity is to raise the anticipation of a wonderful surprise, so make sure your gift looks exciting! Attach a large gift tag that says, "To: [your name]. I love you. [Sign with the name of a friend or spouse.]"

Welcome children and encourage them to sit with others in their Venture Teams. Be sure children know which Venture Team to join and are welcomed warmly.

SAY **It's so exciting to begin our journey together here at The Depot! We'll gather here at the beginning and end of each adventure. Since this is the first week of our adventure, I want to be sure everyone knows what Venture Team they'll be in for this BibleVenture.**

Have each child check his or her name tag or BibleVenture Visa or other list you've created so children know what Venture Teams they're in. Ask children to sit with their Venture Teams during The Depot gathering time.

SAY **We're going to spend the next four weeks learning about how Jesus showed us God's love. Jesus is God's son, and the one reason Jesus came was to show us just how much** (BP) **God loves us.**

Venture view

Establish a nonverbal signal to use to direct kids' attention back to you. Clap your hands, flick the lights, blow a wooden train whistle, or use some other unusual sound maker that won't be mistaken in the midst of discussion. Practice the signal several times until kids recognize and respond to it.

Each week you'll have the opportunity to learn something new about Jesus as you travel to a different Venture Center. And through all our adventures, we'll be reminded that (BP) **God loves us.** We'll also discover some cool ways to share God's love with the people around us. Let me show you what I mean.

Bring out your enormous, gift-wrapped package and show kids. Read the gift tag and show how excited you are to get such a large present.

SAY **Circle up with your BibleVenture Buddy, knee to knee, and discuss:**

● **What could possibly be inside this gift box?**

Ask several teams for their ideas about what might be inside the box.

SAY **Wow, there could be *anything* inside!** [Name of gift giver] **must love me an awful lot to give such a wonderful present. I can't wait to open it! Here I go!** Tear off the wrapping and bring out the bags of candy. **I can't believe it...my very, very favorite candy! And tons of it...all for me. This is enough candy to last me a long time, isn't it?** Pause. **I *could* share it with you guys, though. But then I wouldn't have as much.**

ASK

● **Why would it be a good idea to share this candy with you?**

Call on several children to hear their ideas.

SAY **I really love this kind of candy, but I love you guys even more.** Call up BibleVenture Buddies to retrieve candy bars for their groups. Allow kids to open and enjoy the candy when they get it. While kids are eating, continue: [Name of gift giver] **gave me a gift because he** [or she] **loves me. I wanted to share that gift with you. That reminds me of our Venture Verse. First John 4:11 says, "Dear friends, since God so loved us, we also ought to love one another." Talk about these questions in your Venture Teams:**

● **How is loving others like sharing the candy gift with them?**

● **How is God's love different than a candy bar?**

Allow Venture Teams to discuss the questions, then let each team share some of its responses.

SAY **When I shared this gift, everyone got to enjoy it. God's love isn't something we need to keep to ourselves. It's something he expects us to pass along! God's love is a treasure we can share with everyone we meet. Let's sing a song to remind us how much** (BP) **God loves us and that God's love is an amazing treasure.**

Lead children in singing "I've Found Me a Treasure" (track 1) with the

BibleVentures: Jesus CD. As kids sing the chorus, have them shake hands with kids in other Venture Teams.

SAY **Today you'll learn a lot about how much**  **God loves us. As you're at your Venture Center today, think about ways you can share that amazing love with others. And now, it's time to travel to our Venture Centers!**

Have the leaders of each Venture Center guide the Venture Teams to the area where they'll be meeting. Children will remain at the Venture Centers for forty minutes. When thirty-five minutes have passed, signal the Venture Center Leaders to let them know it's time to wrap up their activities and move children back to The Depot for the closing.

You can find the lyrics to the songs on your *BibleVentures: Jesus* CD on pages 77–79 of this manual.

The Depot: *Closing*

As children begin entering the room, start singing "I've Found Me a Treasure" (track 1) with the CD. Continue singing until all the Venture Teams have returned to The Depot.

SAY **Welcome back to The Depot! I'm sure each of you had an exciting adventure as you learned more about Jesus. And as we learn about how Jesus gave his life for us, we'll remember that**  **God loves us! God showed his love for us by sending Jesus to take away our sins. Jesus was a gift. Our love for God can be like a gift for God.**

Have kids open their Venture Visas to the picture of Jesus riding the donkey into Jerusalem. Ask BibleVenture Buddies to distribute pencils or pens. Encourage kids to think of specific ways they can show that they love God, such as being a friend to someone without friends or sharing a toy with a sibling. Direct kids to write or draw their ideas in the palm leaves on the Venture Visas.

Play "Into My Heart" (track 2) on the CD while kids do this reflective activity. After three minutes, turn off the CD and have BibleVenture Buddies collect pens or pencils.

SAY **Jesus was a gift to us—he showed how much**  **God loves us. Your actions and words can be a gift of love to God too. Think of what you said when you wrote or drew on your paper. Plan to do one of those things this week. Let's talk to God right now and say how much we love him!**

PRAY **Dear God, thank you for the gift of Jesus. Through Jesus' death and resurrection, we have the promise of new life with you. We love you, God, and want to show you our love in so many ways. Guide us as we share your love with others this week. In Jesus' name, amen.**

Ask children to leave their Venture Visas (and name tags if you've created permanent ones) at the ticket window as they leave. Turn on the CD and let those children still waiting for their parents join you in singing a few more songs of praise.

God Loves Us

Venture Verse: "Dear friends, since God so loved us, we also ought to love one another" (1 John 4:11).

Supplies for Week 2

● CD player
● *BibleVentures: Jesus* CD
● pitchers of water
● empty punch bowl
● cookie sheet

The Depot: *Opening*

Welcome children and encourage them to sit with others in their Venture Teams. Be sure that children who were not in class last week know which Venture Team to join and are welcomed warmly.

SAY **We're back to continue our BibleVenture about Jesus. We've been discovering that through Jesus, God showed how much** **God loves us.**

Circle up with your BibleVenture Buddy and discuss:

● **Who are some people you love?**

● **How do you show that you love them?**

After several minutes have passed, continue.

SAY **We've talked about showing *God* how much we love him. But our Venture Verse from 1 John 4:11 reminds us: "Dear friends, since God so loved us, we also ought to love one another." Let's remind *each other* of God's love with this fun activity.**

Start with the Venture Team sitting closest to you. Take the hand of the BibleVenture Buddy and say, "[Name], God loves you." Then pull that person to a standing position. Continue holding the person's hand while you direct him or her to take the hand of a Venture Team member and say, "[Name], God loves you" and pull that child to a standing position.

If your group is smaller than thirty kids, extend this activity by having participants add an action to their "God loves you" statement. Kids can give a high five, shake hands with the person, or give a hug.

When everyone in that team is standing and joining hands, the last person to stand will reach out to another Venture Team to start the process with them. Remind everyone to keep holding hands through the entire experience. Soon everyone will be standing up, holding hands. Lead the group in raising their hands and cheering,  "God loves us!"

Let kids sit down and circle up with their BibleVenture Buddies. Ask teams to discuss:

● **How would this activity have been different if I'd kept the message of God's love to myself?**

● **What happens when we share God's love with others?**

SAY **God loves us so much and expects us to share that love with everyone we meet. When we show God's love to others, it spreads to our homes, schools, sports teams...everywhere!**

God didn't hold any of his love back. He gave it all when he sent Jesus to earth. When we pour out God's love on people around us, they'll start to understand how much God loves them, too. Let's sing a song to praise God and thank him for his love.

Lead children in singing "My God Is" (track 3) with the *BibleVentures: Jesus* CD.

After the song, SAY **As you're at your Venture Center today, think about one way you can share God's love with the people around you. And now, it's time to travel to our Venture Centers!**

Have BibleVenture Buddies guide the Venture Teams assigned to them to the areas where they'll meet. Children will remain at the Venture Centers for forty minutes. When thirty-five minutes have passed, signal the Venture Center Leaders to let them know it's time to wrap up their activities and move children back to The Depot for the closing.

The Depot: *Closing*

Before children arrive, place a punch bowl on a cookie sheet and set it on a table in the front of the room. Set out several pitchers of water.

As children begin entering the room, start singing "I've Found Me a Treasure" (track 1) with the CD. Continue singing until all the teams have returned to The Depot.

SAY **Welcome back to The Depot! I'm sure each of you had an exciting adventure as you learned more about Jesus. And as we learn about how Jesus died for us, we can't help but discover that God loves us!**

BP **God loves us so much, and he showed his love by sending Jesus to take away all the wrong things we do. But God pours out his love to us every day, in other ways, too.** Share one way that God shows his love to you. You might share that you feel God's love when you see a beautiful sunrise, or hear a child's laughter. As you share, pour a bit of water from the pitcher into the punch bowl.

We all feel God's love in different ways, every day. Take turns coming up and saying one way God pours his love into your life. As you share, pour a little water into the bowl. Let kids come forward and share as they pour water into the bowl. Play soft instrumental music during this time (track 12, "Instrumental Music for Prayer Time," is one option).

When everyone has had the opportunity to share and pour water, turn off the CD. Motion to the bowl. SAY **God's love for us overflows! He pours out his love in so many wonderful ways, doesn't he? You've heard lots of ways, but now it's time to write one down. Open your Venture Visas to the page that shows Jesus washing his disciples' feet. On the pitcher of water, write or draw one way that God pours his love into your life every day.**

Allow one minute for kids to draw or write. Gather everyone around the bowl of water for this prayer.

PRAY **Dear Lord, thank you for pouring your love out on us every day. We thank you for sunrises, for laughter, for parents, and all of the ways we feel that you love us. We love you, too, God. Help us to show your love and share it freely with others. In Jesus' name, amen.**

Ask children to leave their Venture Visas (and name tags if you've created permanent ones) at the ticket window as they leave. Turn on the CD and let those children still waiting for their parents join you in singing a few more songs of praise.

If you'd like to extend your time of worship and singing, lead children in singing one or more of the other songs on the *BibleVentures: Jesus* CD.

If you have more than forty kids, you might want to set up two bowls or even give a bowl and pitcher to each Venture Team.

The Depot

God Loves Us

Venture Verse: "Dear friends, since God so loved us, we also ought to love one another" (1 John 4:11).

Supplies for Week 3
● CD player
● *BibleVentures: Jesus* CD
● Bible
● 6-inch squares of wax paper (1 per Venture Team)
● cups of water (1 per Venture Team)
● drinking straws (1 per participant)

The Depot: *Opening*

Welcome children and encourage them to sit in their Venture Teams. Be sure that children who were not in class last week know which Venture Team to join and are welcomed warmly.

SAY **We're back to continue our BibleVenture about Jesus. Let's start by praising God for all of the wonderful things he is and does. As we sing, I want you to make the sign for "I love you"…like this.** Demonstrate how to make the sign for "I love you." Hold up your hand and bend your second and third fingers down. Your thumb, index finger, and pinky should stick straight out. **Every time you sing the word "God," I want you to make the sign for "I love you" and raise your hand high. Ready?** Lead children in singing "My God Is" (track 3) with the *BibleVentures: Jesus* CD.

SAY **God loves us all the time. God even loves us when we make mistakes and do wrong things.** Have everyone stand up. **Sit down if you've ever in your whole life told a lie.** Pause. **Sit down if you've ever—even once—disobeyed your parents.** Pause. **Sit down if you've ever said something that was unkind.** Pause.

Wow! It looks like we've all messed up in our lives…that's called sin. And not one of us is perfect.

Venture view

If you'd like to extend your time of worship and singing, lead children in singing one or more of the other songs on the *BibleVentures: Jesus* CD.

Ask teams to circle up with their BibleVenture Buddies and discuss:

● **Do you think God stops loving us when we sin? Why or why not?**

Have kids stand again and form trios. (Each BibleVenture Buddy should be part of a trio, too.) Direct two kids to join hands, as if they're shaking hands. Instruct the third team member to try and pull their hands apart. Let each trio member have a chance to pull the hands apart. When everyone has had a turn, have kids sit down and in their teams discuss:

● **How hard was it to separate your friends?**

● **What did you do to pull them apart?**

Read aloud Romans 8:38-39 from an easy-to-understand Bible translation. Ask for volunteers to answer these questions:

● **How is this verse like or unlike our activity?**

● **How does it feel to know that nothing in the whole world—or even out of this world—can separate you from God's love?**

My Prayer of Thanks

SAY **We all sin and make mistakes. But it's awesome to know that nothing—not even our sins—has to keep us from God. That's how much**  **God loves us! Because of Jesus, those sins don't have to separate us from God. I'm so thankful for God's love! Take a minute and write a prayer of thanks to God in your Venture Visas.**

Have BibleVenture Buddies distribute pens or pencils, along with the Venture Visas. Allow about two minutes for kids to write a simple prayer of thanks on the page of the visa that shows Jesus in the garden.

SAY **Let's get ready to travel to our Venture Centers to learn more about how Jesus showed God's love to us!**

Have BibleVenture Buddies guide their Venture Teams to the areas where they'll be meeting. Children will remain at the Venture Centers for forty minutes. When thirty-five minutes have passed, signal the Venture Center Leaders to let them know it's time to wrap up their activities and move children back to The Depot for the closing.

The Depot: *Closing*

As children begin entering the room, start singing "Christ Arose" (track 4) with the CD. Continue singing until all the Venture Teams have returned to The Depot.

SAY **Welcome back to The Depot! I'm sure each of you had an exciting adventure as you learned more about Jesus. Earlier we talked about how nothing can keep us from God's love. God forgives us because**  **God loves us so much. Our Venture Verse from 1 John 4:11 reminds us: "Dear friends, since God so loved us, we also ought to love one another."**

Ask teams to circle up with their BibleVenture Buddies and discuss:

● **According to this verse, how should we treat people?**

● **Does God want our love for others to stop when people are unkind to us? Why or why not?**

● **When is it hard to forgive others?**

SAY **Let's do a little experiment to see what happens when we don't forgive others.**

Give each Venture Team a 6-inch square of wax paper, a small cup of water, and enough drinking straws for each person. Direct the BibleVenture Buddies to pour a quarter-sized puddle of water in the center of the wax paper.

Let each team member take turns saying something that a friend might do that is hurtful. For example, kids might say, "You lied to me" or "You called me names." As they share, let kids use a straw as an eyedropper and take a drop of water from the puddle and place it somewhere else on the paper.

Ask BibleVenture Buddies to discuss the following with their teams:

● **What happened to the puddle of water?**

● **How is that like what happens to friends when they don't forgive?**

● **Why does God want us to forgive others?**

Have kids use their straws to blow the water droplets together again. ASK

● **How can God's love change your friendships?**

Call on several volunteers to share their answers. Be careful to not call on the same children too often.

Collect the supplies.

SAY 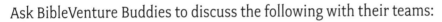 **God loves us and wants us to show his love to everyone around us. That can be hard, especially when others are unkind or unfair. But even when our feelings are hurt, God's love can pull our friendships back together! Let's join together for this prayer.** Have everyone join hands.

PRAY **Heavenly Father, thank you for loving us even when we mess up and sin. Thank you for giving us such a great example of love and forgiveness. Help**

Venture view

Make life easy for your BibleVenture Buddies and yourself by making a copy of the questions for each leader. Then you won't have to keep interrupting the discussion flow to ask the next question.

us to love and forgive our friends and family members with that same love. We want to be like you and do the things that please you. In Jesus' name, amen.

Ask children to leave their Venture Visas (and name tags if you've created permanent ones) at the ticket window as they leave. Turn on the CD and let those children still waiting for their parents join you in singing a few more songs of praise.

The Depot

God Loves Us BP

Venture Verse: "Dear friends, since God so loved us, we also ought to love one another" (1 John 4:11).

Supplies for Week 4

● Bible
● CD player
● *BibleVentures: Jesus* CD
● staplers (1 per Venture Team)
● pens
● slips of paper (3 per participant)

The Depot: *Opening*

Welcome children and encourage them to sit with others in their Venture Teams. Be sure that children who were not in class last week know which Venture Team to join and are welcomed warmly.

SAY **We're back to continue our BibleVenture about Jesus and how he showed us God's love. Because of Jesus, we can be sure that BP God loves us. And our Venture Verse from 1 John 4:11 even reminds us, "Dear friends, since God so loved us, we also ought to love one another."**

● **What people do you think this verse is talking about?**

● **How can you show God's love to the people you just mentioned?**

Call on several volunteers to answer these questions.

SAY **Jesus died on the cross for everyone, to show that God loves all people! Let's make a paper chain to see who some of those people are.**

Give each Venture Team a stapler, pens, and enough strips of paper for each child to have at least three. Direct kids to write the name of someone God loves on each strip of paper. Then have BibleVenture Buddies help kids staple the strips into linking rings to form a paper chain. Have all of the Venture Teams link their chains together to form one long chain. If possible, hang your chain across a wall or from the ceiling.

SAY **Let's do a cheer as we think of all the people that God loves.**

Ask children to think of people they talk to every day who might not know about God's love. Children might think of teachers, friends, coaches, neighbors, and family members.

After a few moments of reflection, ask Venture Teams to each form a circle. Have BibleVenture Buddies start by saying the name of someone who might not know about God's love, and placing a hand in the middle of the circle. Continue to the right, letting each child say a person's name and place a hand in the middle. When each person has both hands in the circle, Venture Teams should cheer, "God loves us!" and raise their hands together. When every team has cheered, continue.

SAY **It's incredible to think that there are people who don't know about God's love. Let's head to our Venture Centers to find out more about God's amazing love.**

Have BibleVenture Buddies guide the Venture Teams to the area where they'll be meeting. Children will remain at the Venture Centers for forty minutes. When thirty-five minutes have passed, signal the Venture Center Leaders to let them know it's time to wrap up their activities and move children back to The Depot for the closing.

The Depot: *Closing*

As children begin entering the room, start singing "I've Found Me a Treasure" (track 1) with the CD. Continue singing until all the Venture Teams have returned to The Depot.

SAY **Welcome back to The Depot! I'm sure each of you had an exciting adventure as you learned more about Jesus. By now each of you has had a chance to travel to all four of the Venture Centers to learn about Jesus and to learn that BP God loves us!**

Motion to the large gift you opened at the first BibleVenture Depot. **You discovered that God's love is a gift.** Point to the paper chains kids made earlier. **And you even thought about all of the people who God loves! As we learned more about Jesus, we also explored a Venture Verse. Let's say it all together.** Lead kids in saying 1 John 4:11, **"Dear friends, since God so loved us, we also ought to love one another."**

If children can't say the verse word for word, decide if that's something you want to stress. Consider having children explain the meaning of the verse to their BibleVenture Buddies, to be sure children understand. It's great if children

If you'd like to extend your time of worship and singing, lead children in singing one or more of the songs on the *BibleVentures: Jesus* CD.

can quote the verse word for word, but not at the expense of understanding and being able to explain the meaning of the verse.

Have children circle up with their BibleVenture Buddies and discuss:

● **What are some ways God shows his love for you?**

● **Why do you think God sent Jesus?**

● **What's one thing you've learned through this BibleVenture that you can tell someone at home or at school?**

Direct kids to open their Venture Visas to the page that shows the cross with hearts around it. Distribute pencils or pens, and ask kids to think of other people who need to know of God's love.

SAY **Jesus died for all of us! God loves all of us! Take a minute and write the names of people who Jesus died for. As you do, think of a way you can tell that person about God's amazing love.**

Make life easy for your BibleVenture Buddies and yourself by making a copy of the questions for each leader. Then you won't have to keep interrupting the discussion flow to ask the next question.

As kids work, play "Into My Heart" (track 2) on the CD. When the song ends, turn off the CD.

SAY **As you leave today, take your Venture Visas with you. This booklet will be a reminder of the travels you've had in this BibleVenture on Jesus. And it can remind you that God loves you very much!**

Have children remain in their Venture Teams and pray for each other. Ask children to pray that God would help them share his love with others, and to remember all that Jesus did for them. After a couple of minutes, begin softly playing "Christ Arose" (track 4) on the CD to signal that it's time to finish praying.

SAY **Let's praise God for all we've learned and for his incredible love!**

Have children stand and join you in singing any of the songs on the CD. Continue singing and praising God as parents arrive to pick up their children.

Alternate Opening or Closing for The Depot

If one of the activities for the Opening or Closing in The Depot won't work for your setting or facility, you can substitute this idea...

Have a congregation member bring in a variety of pets he or she owns. Let the person talk about all they do to care for their pets—feeding them, cleaning up after them, training them, and taking them to the vet. Talk about how God shows his love for us—by providing all we need, forgiving us, disciplining us, and giving us a church where we can learn more about him.

Venture Center One:

God Loves Us

Venture Verse: "Dear friends, since God so loved us, we also ought to love one another" (1 John 4:11).

Welcome!

You'll be leading the Games Venture Center for the next four weeks.

One great piece of news is that preparing for the four weeks is easy because you prepare just *one* week's lesson—and present it four times!

Here's how your Venture Center works: Each week children gather at The Depot for a time of opening and adventure. While at The Depot, children will get together in their Venture Teams, and then one group (it could be one Venture Team or several, but each will have an adult leader) will travel to your Venture Center.

This group of children will stay with you for forty minutes, then return to The Depot for a time of closing and celebration.

In the weeks that follow, different groups of children will come to your Venture Center. You'll repeat the same activity all four weeks, each week with a different group of children. This allows you to prepare just once and have four weeks of meaningful interaction with children as you lead them closer to God!

Your Venture Center

During this BibleVenture, children will dig into the story of Jesus' last week on earth. Children will learn that  God loves us and showed that love through the sacrifice of Christ.

In your Venture Center, children will use games to explore the excitement and joy of Jesus' triumphal entry into Jerusalem.

Children *love* to play games. But too often game time is also when kids discover that they're not fast enough, not tall enough, and not as coordinated as everyone else. And anyone who has been picked last for a softball game knows how humiliation feels.

That's why your role in leading this Venture Center is so important. You'll

These games were written *specifically* to help children explore the Bible accounts. When you use these activities, game time becomes learning time, too!

make sure that game time is positive, that everybody plays, that everybody cooperates, and that nobody goes home feeling like a loser.

The goal is for kids to play *with* one another, not *against* one another. It's a new concept for some children—and adults, too.

Your enthusiasm for this Venture Center and the games will be passed on to the children you meet each week. Greet them with excitement, encourage them to join in the games, and have fun!

Preparation

Before children arrive, gather these supplies:

- CD player
- *BibleVentures: Jesus CD*
- Bible
- paper grocery sacks (1 per 10 children)
- scissors
- Mylar strips
- masking tape
- bandannas (1 per 10 children)
- clock or watch with a second hand
- yellow, green, and red construction paper
- parachute or king-size bedsheet
- 1 highlighter for each Venture Group

Prepare your playing area by using masking tape to make a twisty path about six to eight feet long on the ground. The path should be about three feet across, so children can walk down it.

Cut one side out of a paper grocery sack to create an opening for a face. Tape or glue Mylar strips to the center of the top and back of the sack to resemble a donkey's mane. Create one of these for each group of ten children.

Cut out a simple crown pattern from the yellow paper, a palm leaf from the green paper, and a heart from the red paper. You'll need one set of shapes for each Venture Team.

The Venture Center

Welcome children as they enter your Venture Center. Explain that kids will explore the story of Jesus' triumphal entry through games.

SAY **Jesus had been teaching about God, doing incredible miracles, and sharing God's love. People were amazed at Jesus! They'd never seen or heard**

Establish a nonverbal signal to use to direct kids' attention back to you. Clap your hands, flick the lights, or use a wooden train whistle or other unusual sound-maker that won't be mistaken in the midst of discussion. Practice the signal several times until kids recognize it and respond to it.

of anyone like him. Some people even thought Jesus was the king that God's people had been waiting for. Listen to what happened when Jesus was coming to Jerusalem.

Read aloud John 12:12-15. Explain that *Hosanna* means "save."

Ask children to circle up with their BibleVenture Buddies and discuss:

● **Why were people excited to see Jesus?**

● **Why did the people call for Jesus to save them?**

SAY **When Jesus rode into Jerusalem, the people were so excited! Let's play a game to see how exciting it was that day.**

Chase the Donkey's Tail

SAY **In this game, all of your Venture Teams will join together to form one giant "donkey."** Have kids all face the same direction in a row and hold hands. Be sure your donkeys are made up of no more than ten children.

Give the first person in line the donkey's head you prepared earlier. Give the last person in line a bandanna to tuck into his or her waistband or a pocket, as a tail.

SAY [Name of first child] **will be the Head of our donkey, and** [name of last child] **will be the Tail. The donkey Head will have fifteen seconds to try to grab the donkey Tail—the bandanna—without breaking the line apart.**

After you hear me call "time," if the Head grabbed the bandanna, everyone must give the Head high fives. If the Tail kept the bandanna safe, everyone must give the Tail high fives. After the high fives, the Head must give the donkey's head to someone else and the Tail must give the donkey's tail to someone else. Those people will become the new Head and Tail. I'd like you to give the head and tail to someone who's not on your Venture Team.

Call "time" at fifteen-second intervals. For extra fun play "Donkey Braying" (track 9) on the CD. It's fifteen seconds long; when the track ends, you'll know to call "time."

Play several times so many kids get to be the Head and Tail. Then collect the donkey head and bandanna, and have kids form knee-to-knee circles with their Venture Teams. Have Venture Teams discuss the following questions together:

● **What was fun about this game?**

● **In today's Bible story, what do you think was fun about welcoming Jesus to Jerusalem?**

Make life easy for your BibleVenture Buddies and yourself by making a copy of the questions for each leader. Then you won't have to keep interrupting the discussion flow to ask the next question.

● **How do you think Jesus felt as he heard people praising him?**

SAY **The donkey in our Bible story carried Jesus into Jerusalem. We can't carry Jesus, but as Jesus' followers, we can carry an important message about God:** 🅱🅿 **God loves us. Let's remember to carry that message to our friends this week.**

The people who praised Jesus were happy because they thought Jesus was going to lead them, like a king. Let's play a game to learn some of the things people thought about Jesus.

Jesus Is...

Have Venture Teams remain in their circles. Join a Venture Team to explain and demonstrate the game.

SAY **The people who came to praise and welcome Jesus that day had heard many things about him.** Hold up the paper crown. **They'd heard that Jesus was their king.** Hold up the paper heart. **Some had heard that Jesus was the Son of God. This heart will remind us of our loving God.** Hold up the paper palm leaf. **Some people heard that Jesus was Lord—the Messiah who would come to save them. That's why they waved palm leaves that day.**

Turn to the person on your right and hold out the crown.

SAY **When I hand you the crown, I'll say, "Jesus is the king," and you'll say, "The what?" I'll say, "The king," and you'll say, "The what?" Again I'll say, "The king." Finally, you'll say, "Oh, the king!" and take the crown from me.**

Practice running through the "script" once or twice, then instruct the person on your right to take the crown and continue the pattern with the person on his or her right. The crown will continue around the circle until everyone has had a turn.

SAY **Now the game will get tricky! When someone hands you the heart, he or she will say, "Jesus is the Son" to remind you that Jesus is God's son. We'll play the same game with the heart. We'll also add in the palm leaf, saying, "Jesus is Lord." As each piece is added in, you'll have to talk to people on both sides of you in order to pass on the information with the paper pieces.**

Have the BibleVenture Buddies start the paper pieces and the script in each circle. Sound confusing? At first, maybe. But your kids will soon catch on that when the person on their right says, "The what?" they'll respond by turning to the person on their left and saying "The what?"

After playing for a minute or two, collect the paper shapes. Have Venture Teams discuss the following questions together:

● **How did you feel when you played this game? Why?**

● **How is that like the way Jesus' friends might have felt when they heard people calling Jesus a king?**

● **What does it mean to make Jesus the king of your life?**

SAY **God's people wanted a king who would help them fight their enemies. They wanted a king who was like them and who would make them a mighty nation. But Jesus didn't come to be that kind of king. Jesus wants to be king of your heart—the most important thing in your life. Because**  **God loves us, we can make Jesus the most important thing every day. And Jesus will help us through hard or confusing times. Let's play another exciting game to see what that's like.**

Rocky Road

Lead children to the twisty path you made on the ground. SAY **When Jesus entered Jerusalem, the road was lined with people shouting things. They shouted "Hosanna" and "Blessed is he who comes in the name of the Lord" and "Blessed is the King of Israel!" Those were great things to shout! In this game, some of you will shout good, helpful things. Others will shout things that won't be so helpful.**

Form two teams. Blindfold one child with a bandanna. Have kids stand on both sides of the path. Mix up the two teams so there are members of each team standing on either side of the path. Tell the members of the blindfolded child's team that it is their job to get their teammate safely through the path. They can shout out directions, but they cannot touch their teammate in any way. As soon as their teammate steps on a masking-tape line, he or she is out. Tell the opposing team that its job is to confuse the blindfolded person by shouting out directions that will make him or her step on the line.

Position the blindfolded child at the start of the path, then call "go." Allow everyone a chance to try "navigating" the path. Then choose a person to be blindfolded, but this time choose another person to act as a guide. The guide will not be blindfolded and will act as the spokesperson for his or her team. The guide will give directions but cannot touch the child. The opposing team will still try to confuse the child by shouting out incorrect directions.

After each child has gone through the course with a guide, have kids sit down in a circle with their BibleVenture Buddies to discuss:

Since this game becomes challenging if it's played too fast, encourage BibleVenture Buddies to keep the pace slow and steady. A steady rhythm will help children master the game. If you do decide to play a speeded up round, play "Fast and Faster" (track 10) on the CD. It's ninety seconds of music that gradually speeds up, then stops.

● Which was easier, walking though the path alone or with a guide? Explain.

● Tell about a time people around you wanted you to do something that was wrong.

● How is Jesus like a guide to you?

SAY **When Jesus rode into Jerusalem, lots of people wanted to follow him and join the celebration. But when things got tough, hardly anyone wanted to follow Jesus. BP God loves us and knows that sometimes life can be confusing or hard. He knows that people will sometimes want us to do things that aren't right. That's why God gave us Jesus! By staying close to Jesus, you and I can have a guide to lead us through hard times. Let's play a game and celebrate God's love right now!**

Parachute Palms

SAY **When Jesus entered Jerusalem, people waved palm branches. In this game, we'll wave a parachute!**

Spread out the parachute or king-size bedsheet and have kids form a circle around it, holding onto the edge. Have kids practice lifting the parachute in unison until their arms are extended over their heads and then quickly pulling it down to the ground.

SAY **As you lift up the parachute, I'll call out something that describes you, such as "brown hair" or "wearing tennis shoes." If I call out something that describes you, run under the parachute while it's in the air and yell, "God loves you!" to the other kids under there with you. Then run out from under the parachute as fast as you can so you don't get trapped when everyone else pulls it to the ground.**

As kids are lifting the parachute, call out descriptors such as

● January birthdays

● wearing blue

● born on an even-numbered day

● have Velcro on their shoes

● go to a particular school

● like to eat vegetables

End the game by calling "everyone!" The parachute will fly into the air, and no one will be caught.

Many schools, preschools, or day care centers have parachutes you might be able to borrow. Check around to see if you can find one—it'll make this game extra fun!

SAY **Just as the parachute flew into the air, I want you to fly out of here bursting with excitement about God's love.** (BP) **God loves us! Remember how the people were so excited to praise and honor Jesus? This week, look for ways you can joyfully share God's love with people around you.**

Start right now by opening up your visas to the page that shows Jesus riding on a donkey. In your Venture Groups, take turns using the highlighter to make a heart on a neighbor's page as a reminder of God's love and how we can share it with others.

When children finish this, it should be about time to move back to The Depot. Close your Venture Center with a short prayer, thanking God for sending Jesus to show his love. Then help BibleVenture Buddies escort the children back to The Depot for the closing.

If you still have time....
If you finish before it's time to head back to The Depot, use this activity.

Explain that in today's Bible story, people waved palm branches to honor and praise Jesus. Point out that in this activity, kids will wave palms too—their own palms (or hands!). Have kids form two lines, facing each other about five feet apart, and hold out one palm. Choose one child to stand at the head of the path. Spin the child around ten times, then direct him or her to walk down the path and give high fives to the outstretched palms. Kids will have a silly, dizzy time trying to stay on the path!

Venture Center Two:

God Loves Us BP

Venture Verse: "Dear friends, since God so loved us, we also ought to love one another" (1 John 4:11).

Welcome!

You'll be leading the Storytelling Venture Center for the next four weeks.

One great piece of news is that preparing for the four weeks is easy because you prepare just *one* week's lesson—and present it four times!

Here's how your Venture Center works: Each week children gather at The Depot for a time of opening and adventure. While at The Depot, children will get together in their Venture Teams, and then one group (it could be one Venture Team or several, but each will have an adult leader) will travel to your Venture Center.

This team of children will stay with you for forty minutes, then return to The Depot for a time of closing and celebration.

In the weeks that follow, different groups of children will come to your Venture Center. You'll repeat the same activity for all four weeks, each week with a different group of children. This allows you to prepare just once and have four weeks of meaningful interaction with children as you lead them closer to God!

Your Venture Center

During this BibleVenture, children will dig into the story of Jesus' last supper with his disciples. Children will learn that BP God loves us and showed that love through the sacrifice of Christ.

You'll notice that the Bible Point, *God loves us*, is mentioned several times in your lesson. That's by intent, and it's important you reinforce the Point by saying it each time—or even more often. By the end of this BibleVenture, children will have discovered how God demonstrated his love and how they can share that love with one another.

In your Venture Center, children will take part in a Passover (or seder) meal just as Jesus and his friends would have done.

Preparation

Before children arrive, gather these supplies:

- large pitchers of warm water
- large washbasin or plastic bin
- several towels
- blanket large enough for all groups to sit around
- large pillows (ideally, 1 per person)
- matzo crackers (enough for everyone to have some)
- grape juice
- 1 or 2 hard-boiled eggs in a bowl
- small bowl of haroseth (see recipe in box)
- small bowl of parsley
- small bowl of saltwater
- bone from a turkey leg or other kind of meat
- small bowl of horseradish
- small paper cups
- plates
- large platter
- highlighter

Venture view

To make haroseth, finely chop two apples and place them in a bowl. Add ⅓ cup chopped walnuts and 2 teaspoons of cinnamon.

Before children arrive, gather the supplies listed above for your Passover (or seder) meal. Set the supplies on a table, off to the side. Kids will help you set up the Passover meal on the floor, so clear away any other classroom items that might be a distraction.

The Venture Center

Welcome children to your Venture Center. Introduce yourself, then ask if anyone has ever heard of Passover.

SAY **A long time ago, God's people were slaves in Egypt. They had to work very hard and do whatever the king—called Pharaoh—said to do. But God sent Moses to help lead the Israelites to freedom. Jews today still celebrate a special holiday called Passover. It's a time for them to remember God's love and how he freed them.**

The Bible tells us about a time Jesus and his friends gathered to celebrate the Passover meal together. Jesus' friends didn't know it, but this would be

Venture view

Establish a nonverbal signal to use to direct kids' attention back to you. Clap your hands, flick the lights, or use a wooden train whistle or other unusual sound-maker that won't be mistaken in the midst of discussion. Practice the signal several times until kids recognize it and respond to it.

the last time they would get to be with Jesus. Jesus told his friends to go into Jerusalem and make all the preparations for the meal. Today you'll help me get ready for that special Passover.**

Direct children to take off their shoes and socks and set them against a wall, or outside the door. Point out that in Jesus' time, people wore sandals or even went barefoot.

SAY **First, we'll need a place to sit and eat.** Direct two kids to spread the blanket in the center of the room. Let each person get a pillow and set it around the edges of the blanket.

When the Israelites left Egypt, they had to leave very quickly. There wasn't time to let their bread rise to get nice and fluffy. To remember that, we'll have matzo—it's bread without yeast. Bring out the matzo, and let a child place the plate of matzo on a large platter in the center of the blanket.

At Passover, Jews eat some special foods. Each food reminds them of something different. Bring out the bowl of haroseth and pass it around so kids can smell it and see it. **This is called haroseth.**

Ask the following questions and let several volunteers answer:

● **What does it smell like?**

● **What does this look like?**

SAY **Haroseth looks a little like mushy cement. The Israelites had to use something like cement to make bricks to build things for the Pharaoh. So the haroseth reminds them of the hard work they did, building things for the Pharaoh.** Set the bowl of haroseth on the platter.

Bring out the bowl of parsley and the bowl of saltwater and pass them around. Let kids smell the parsley and dip a finger in the saltwater to taste it.

SAY **This parsley is green, which reminds the Jews of springtime—when they celebrate Passover. Dip your finger in the water and tell me what it tastes like.** Let kids respond. **The water is salty...like our tears.**

Ask children to discuss at their "tables:"

● **What might the salty water remind them of?**

SAY **The salty water reminds them of all the tears the Israelites shed when they were slaves. Remember, God's people had to work hard and didn't have their own country. That must have made them really sad.** Set the parsley and saltwater on the platter.

Bring out the hard-boiled eggs and pass them around.

If you have a large group of children, have several teams work together to create a blanket "table" and provide an appropriate number of serving dishes.

SAY **Many of us dye eggs at Easter. Eggs are a symbol of springtime and new life. The eggs remind Jews that Passover comes in the spring.** Set the eggs on the platter.

Bring out the bone and pass it around. Let children touch it and smell it. Ask several volunteers to suggest answers for the following questions:

- **What is this?**

- **Why do you think they set this out at Passover?**

SAY **This bone is a reminder of the sacrificial lamb. When the Israelites were in Egypt, God told them to kill a lamb—a perfect lamb—as a sacrifice or special offering to God. They spread the blood of the lamb on the doorposts of their homes. That night, God sent an angel through Egypt. If the angel saw blood on the doorpost, the people inside were safe. If there wasn't blood on the doorpost, the firstborn inside the house would die.**

Ask tables of children (up to two teams) to discuss:

- **Why is it important to remember the sacrificial lamb?**

Set the bone on the platter. Bring out the horseradish and pass it around so kids can smell it.

SAY **This is horseradish—a bitter herb. Remember, the Israelites worked very hard in Egypt and went through many hard times. The bitter herbs remind them of their bitter afflictions—the sad and hard things they went though.**

Ask tables of children to discuss:

- **How did this meal help the Jews remember God's love?**

- **Why do you think Jesus wanted to have Passover with his friends?**

SAY **It looks like we're almost ready for our Passover meal! Jesus' friends probably drank wine with their meal, but we'll just have grape juice.** Ask the BibleVenture Buddies to help pour a small amount of grape juice for each child in his or her Venture Team.

Before Jesus and his friends ate, Jesus broke the bread. Break the matzo into smaller pieces. **He told the disciples, "This is my body given for you; do this in remembrance of me."** As you distribute the pieces of matzo, ask tables to answer the following question:

- **What do you think Jesus meant when he said that?**

SAY **Then, Jesus took a cup of wine and said that the wine was like his blood. That sounds kind of gross, doesn't it?**

Ask tables to discuss:

● **What do you think Jesus meant when he said that?**

SAY **Jesus was giving the disciples clues that his body was going to be broken—his blood was going to be shed. Jesus was going to die soon. Just as they were gathered to remember God's love with the Passover, Jesus wanted his friends to remember him, too.**

Play "Jesus Is All the World to Me" (track 5) on the *BibleVentures: Jesus* CD. Let children eat their matzo and drink their juice as they listen to the song.

Turn off the CD.

SAY **After the meal, Jesus did something very surprising. He got up and took off the outer part of his robe. Then he wrapped a towel around his waist.** Get up and wrap a towel around your waist. Get the water pitchers and basin. Kneel before one child and pour a little water into the basin. **Jesus poured some water into a basin and began to wash the disciples' feet. Let's see what that was like.**

Have each BibleVenture Buddy get a basin, pitcher, and towel. Let the Venture Teams circle up and direct the BibleVenture Buddies to wash and dry the feet of each group member. While kids participate in the foot-washing activity, play "Instrumental Music for Prayer Time" (track 12) on the CD. When everyone has had a turn, gather everyone together. Ask several volunteers to answer:

● **What was it like to have someone wash your feet?**

● **What do you think it was like for the disciples?**

● **How did this show God's love?**

● **Jesus showed love by doing something a servant would do...washing feet. Circle up with your BibleVenture Buddy and share one specific way you can show God's love to your friends at school or in your neighborhood.**

SAY **The Passover meal was a chance for Jesus to show his love—God's love—for his friends.** **BP** **God loves us so much that he sent Jesus. When Jesus was on earth, he served, taught, healed, and loved people. Jesus was God's gift of love for you and for me. This special meal helps us remember that** **BP** **God loves us.**

When children finish, it should be about time to move back to The Depot. Close with prayer, thanking God for the plans he has for each child, and asking him to give strength to each child as it's needed. Then escort the children back to The Depot for the closing.

For extra fun, use a spray water bottle to add "atmosphere" as kids are acting.

If you still have time....

If you finish before it's time to head back to The Depot, use the following activity.

SAY **Jesus knew it was almost time for him to die. He wouldn't be with his disciples much longer.** Ask teams to circle up and discuss:

● **What would you do if you knew you wouldn't see your friends much longer?**

● **How is that like or unlike what Jesus did?**

SAY **Jesus loved and served his friends. Find a partner on your Venture Team, and tell one way you'll plan to serve your friends or family this week.**

Allow five minutes for partners to share. Then call on each pair to tell some of the ideas they talked about. Close with a prayer, asking God to help us serve others and share his love the way Jesus did.

Venture Center Three:

God Loves Us 🅱️🅿️

Venture Verse: "Dear friends, since God so loved us, we also ought to love one another" (1 John 4:11).

Welcome!

You'll be leading the Art Venture Center for the next four weeks.

One great piece of news is that preparing for the four weeks is easy because you prepare just *one* week's lesson—and present it four times!

Here's how your Venture Center works: Each week children gather at The Depot for a time of opening and adventure. While at The Depot, children will get together in their Venture Teams, and then one group (it could be one Venture Team or several, but each will have an adult leader) will travel to your Venture Center.

This group of children will stay with you for forty minutes, then return to The Depot for a time of closing and celebration.

In the weeks that follow, different groups of children will come to your Venture Center. You'll repeat the same activity all four weeks, each week with a different group of children. This allows you to prepare just once and have four weeks of meaningful interaction with children as you lead them closer to God!

Your Venture Center

During this BibleVenture, children will explore how Jesus prayed in the Garden of Gethsemane, and how 🅱️🅿️ God loves us.

You'll notice that the Bible Point, *God loves us,* is mentioned several times in your lesson. That's by intent, and it's important you reinforce the Point by saying it each time—or even more often. By the end of this BibleVenture, children will have discovered how God demonstrated his love and how they can share that love with one another.

In your Venture Center, children will use their creative skills to craft a prayer bracelet that will remind them how to pray and who they can pray for.

Children will be able to use their bracelets as tools to connect with God in new and powerful ways.

Your enthusiasm for this Venture Center and the craft will be passed on to the children you meet each week. Greet them with excitement, encourage them to join in the activity, and have fun!

Preparation

Before children arrive, gather these supplies:
- highlighter
- Bible
- 12-inch lengths of leather lacing
- wooden beads in the following colors: green, yellow, red, black, blue, white
- scissors
- CD player
- *BibleVentures: Jesus* CD
- markers
- photocopies of the "Prayer Bracelet" handout (p. 63)

Before kids arrive, make a sample bracelet and wear it. Set all of the supplies in the middle of your room, placing the beads in small bowls.

The Venture Center

Welcome children as they enter your Venture Center. Explain that kids will explore the story of how Jesus prayed in the Garden of Gethsemane, and will make a bracelet to help them as they pray too. Have children form a large circle around the art supplies.

SAY **First, I want you to try something. I'm going to give the BibleVenture Buddies a special message. They'll share the message with you, but there's a catch: They can't talk or make any noise at all.**

Call the BibleVenture Buddies up front and give them a message such as "You kids are great! I really like you!" or "The kids in this class are awesome." Give them two minutes to share the message with their teams without speaking. Call time.

Ask teams to circle up with their BibleVenture Buddies and discuss:

- **What were your leaders trying to tell you?**

- **What was it like to try and figure out what they were saying?**

Establish a nonverbal signal to use to direct kids' attention back to you. Clap your hands, flick the lights, blow a wooden train whistle, or use another unusual sound maker that won't be mistaken in the midst of discussion. Practice the signal several times until kids recognize it and respond to it.

SAY **It would have been a lot easier if our BibleVenture Buddies had just told you their special message. Sometimes it's good to show people what we mean, but it's also great to just *say* what we mean.**

In today's Bible story, Jesus spent some time talking to God—we call that *prayer*. Jesus knew that it was almost time for him to be arrested. His time on earth was almost over, and he was facing something really hard. So he went where it was quiet and talked to God. This is what Jesus said. Read aloud John 17:1. Ask for a volunteer or two to answer the following question:

● **Why would Jesus want to talk to his father?**

SAY **Jesus prayed that God would give him the strength to die for our sins. He knew that would be hard—and painful—to do! But he also knew it was the right thing to do. Let's see what else Jesus said.** Read aloud John 17:14-15. Ask children to circle up with their BibleVenture Buddies and discuss:

● **Who do you think Jesus is talking about?**

● **Why did he pray for his friends?**

SAY **Jesus prayed for his disciples because he knew things would be hard for them, too. If the disciples got so scared that they wouldn't talk about God, then no one could help people know about God! So Jesus wanted God to protect and care for the disciples. Let's see what else Jesus said.** Read aloud John 17:20-21. Ask for a volunteer or two to answer the following question:

● **Who is Jesus talking about in this part of his prayer?**

SAY **Jesus prayed for the people who would come to believe in him...like you and me.** Discuss these questions with your BibleVenture Buddies:

● **How does it feel to know that Jesus prayed for you before you were even born?**

● **Why do you think God wants us to pray?**

SAY 🔵 **God loves us and loves for us to talk to him. God is pleased when we show that we love him—by using kind words, by loving others, by going to church, and by reading God's Word. But there's nothing like speaking to God to tell him how we feel. Or to pray for others like Jesus did.**

Let's make a prayer bracelet and think of all the people we can pray for—and thank God for!

Let BibleVenture Buddies retrieve enough 12-inch lengths of leather lacing for each child in the group.

Make life easy for your BibleVenture Buddies and yourself by making a copy of the questions for each leader. Then you won't have to keep interrupting the discussion flow to ask the next question.

SAY **Start by tying a knot at one end of your lace. This knot will hold the beads in place. It will also remind us that we're held tightly in the loving arms of our heavenly Father. You'll tie lots of knots as you make your bracelet. Each knot is a reminder that (BP) God loves us. Think of the knot like a little hug!** Pause while kids tie a knot at the end of the lacing. Be sure kids leave a 2-inch "tail" at the end so they can tie the ends of the bracelet together.

First, we'll put a green bead on the bracelet. Ask several volunteers to answer the following question:

● **What does green remind you of?**

SAY **Green will remind us of young people, because there's so much green in spring—when life is new. Let the youngest person in your group come get one green bead for each person. As you add the green bead, think of all the young people—children—you can pray for.** Pause while kids retrieve the green beads and add them to their bracelets. **Now, add a knot to remember that (BP) God loves us and God loves young people.** Pause while kids tie a knot after the green bead.

Next, we'll add a yellow bead to the bracelet. Ask several volunteers to answer the following question:

● **What does yellow make you think of?**

SAY **Yellow will remind us to be like a light, shining God's love. Let the person in your group who is happiest today get one yellow bead for each person. As you add the yellow bead, think of a way you can shine the light of God's love.** Pause while kids retrieve the yellow beads and add them to their bracelets. **Now, add a knot to remember that (BP) God loves us and we can share that love by being a light to those around us.** Pause while kids tie a knot after the yellow bead.

Next, we'll add a red bead to the bracelet. Ask several volunteers to answer the following question:

● **What does red remind you of?**

SAY **Red is often used on hearts or valentines. So red will remind us of all the people who love us. Decide which group member has shown love today, and let him or her get the red beads for your group. As you add the red bead, think of all the people who love you.** Pause while kids retrieve the red beads and add them to their bracelets. **Now, add a knot to remember that (BP) God loves us and has surrounded us with loving friends and family members.** Pause while kids tie a knot after the red bead.

Our next bead is black. Ask several volunteers to answer the following question:

● **What does black remind you of?**

SAY **Sometimes, dark colors remind us of sadness or darkness. Jesus once said that people in the world were living in darkness because they didn't have the light of God. So black will remind us of all the people who don't know God. Send someone who is wearing black to get the black beads for your group. As you add the black bead, think of all the people who don't know God.** Pause while kids retrieve the black beads and add them to their bracelets. **Now, add a knot to remember that** (BP) **God loves us—even people who don't know or love him.** Pause while kids tie a knot after the black bead.

Next, we'll add a blue bead to the bracelet. Ask several volunteers to answer the following question:

● **What does blue make you think of?**

SAY **Sometimes when people are sad, we say they're blue. So the blue bead will remind us to pray for people who are sad. See if anyone in your group felt sad this week. Send that person forward to get blue beads for the group. As you add the blue bead, think of all the sad people in our world.** Pause while kids retrieve the blue beads and add them to their bracelets. **Now, add a knot to remember that** (BP) **God loves us and wants to comfort us when we're sad.** Pause while kids tie a knot after the blue bead.

Finally, we'll add a white bead to the bracelet. Ask several volunteers to answer the following question:

● **What are some things that are white?**

SAY **When people get old, sometimes their hair turns white. So white will remind us of all the old people we can pray for. Let the oldest person in your group come up and take one white bead for each person. As you add the white bead, think of all the older people you can pray for.** Pause while kids retrieve the white beads and add them to their bracelets. **Now, add a knot to remember that** (BP) **God loves us and loves older people, too.** Pause while kids tie a knot after the white bead.

Before we wear these, I want each person to make a little reminder of what each bead represents. Distribute markers and the "Prayer Bracelet" handouts. Have kids color each bead on the handout, then write the names of people they think of in each category. For example, near the white bead, kids might write "Grandma and Grandpa," or "My teacher, Mr. Collins." Near the yellow bead, direct kids to write specific ways they can be a light—someone who shows others what it's like to follow God.

During this time, play soft music. "Quiet Music" (track 11) on the CD is a good option. Set your CD player on "repeat" so the track plays again and again as your children work.

Allow kids about five minutes to work on the handouts, then gather the markers.

SAY **Now form a circle with your Venture Team. Let the person on your right tie the ends of your bracelet together. As you tie the knot, think of how prayer ties us—or connects us—to God. Jesus wanted to be connected to God when he was sad. He wanted to remember how much God loved him. As you tie the knot for your friend, say "God loves you,** [name of person]." Pause while kids (and leaders) tie the bracelets on each other. Have scissors on hand so kids can cut off any excess lacing.

When everyone is wearing a bracelet, ask kids to scatter around the room so they're not sitting near anyone. Explain that they're going to have a chance to use the bracelets right now in prayer. Play "Instrumental Music for Prayer Time" (track 12) on the CD while kids touch each bead and pray for the people represented by each color. When the song ends, turn off the CD.

SAY **Long, long before we were born, Jesus prayed for us. Jesus knew that it would be hard to follow God sometimes. He loved you so much that he lifted you up before God. As you use your bracelet to pray for others and thank God for them, remember that (BP) God loves us.**

When children finish this, it should be about time to move back to The Depot. Escort the children back to The Depot for the closing.

If you still have time....
If you finish before it's time to head back to The Depot, use the following activity.

Have each Venture Team form a circle. Let the BibleVenture Buddy begin by saying, "God, I thank you for..." and add something that starts with the letter A. The next person will say, "God, I thank you for..." and add something that begins with the letter B. Continue around the circle and let kids thank God for things that begin with each letter of the alphabet. When they reach Z, have kids shout "amen" together.

Prayer Bracelet

Green

I can pray for or thank God for these kids: _____.

Yellow

I can be a light by _____.

Red

I can pray for or thank God for these people who love me: _____.

Black

I can pray for these people who don't know God: _____.

Blue

I can pray for these people who are sad: _____.

White

I can pray for or thank God for these older people: _____.

Venture Center Four:

God Loves Us BP

Venture Verse: "Dear friends, since God so loved us, we also ought to love one another" (1 John 4:11).

Welcome!

You'll be leading the Drama Venture Center for the next four weeks.

One great piece of news is that preparing for the four weeks is easy because you prepare just *one* week's lesson—and present it four times!

Here's how your Venture Center works: Each week children gather at The Depot for a time of opening and adventure. While at The Depot, children will get together in their Venture Teams, and then one group (it could be one Venture Team or several, but each will have an adult leader) will travel to your Venture Center.

This group of children will stay with you for forty minutes, and then return to The Depot for a time of closing and celebration.

In the weeks that follow, different groups of children will come to your Venture Center. You'll repeat the same activity all four weeks, each week with a different group of children. This allows you to prepare just once and have four weeks of meaningful interaction with children as you lead them closer to God!

Your Venture Center

During this BibleVenture, children will dig into the story of Jesus' last week on earth. Children will learn that BP God loves us and showed that love through the sacrifice of Christ.

You'll notice that the Bible Point, *God loves us*, is mentioned several times in your lesson. That's by intent, and it's important you reinforce the Point by saying it each time—or even more often.

In your Venture Center, children will use drama to explore Jesus' death and resurrection. There's no memorizing lines or turning script pages; children simply listen to sections of the CD as directed in the lesson, and act along with the instructions they hear on the CD.

The drama takes place in two episodes. Between the episodes you'll lead children in several discussion sessions. You may also choose to switch roles in your cast between episodes. Some of the roles require more action and participation than others, but it's important for every child to have an opportunity to participate in a role.

Your enthusiasm for this Venture Center and the drama will be passed on to the children you meet each week. Greet them with excitement, encourage them to join the drama, and have fun!

Preparation

Before children arrive, gather these supplies:
- CD player
- *BibleVentures: Jesus* CD
- highlighter
- 2 toy microphones (or props to represent microphones)
- paper palm leaves
- scarves or towels
- photocopies of the "Breaking News!" handout
- crayons or markers
- Bible costumes (optional)

The scripts that match what you'll hear on the CD are included in this leader guide, beginning on page 71. You will *not* need to provide these for the children, as there are no parts to read or memorize. The script is provided for your reference. Listen to the CD one time before your first meeting so you're familiar with the various roles and breaks in the drama.

Set up the stage area. This may be one side of the room, or an actual stage. If there are children who do not wish to participate, they may sit in your audience. However, try to encourage everyone to participate, even if it's in a small role.

The Venture Center

Welcome children as they enter your Venture Center. Explain that kids will explore Jesus' death and resurrection through a drama, and will put on the drama themselves!

SAY **We're going to learn about something amazing that Jesus did through an instant drama. Each of you will have the opportunity to participate in this drama. Our drama has two parts, then a fun wrap-up rap! After the first section, we'll have time for discussion and to change our cast.**

Some children are simply too shy to participate in a drama. If you have a very shy child, encourage him or her to be part of a sound effects crew. Also, if you have a very large class, you could let some of the students be on the sound effects crew as well.

Establish a nonverbal signal to use to direct kids' attention back to you. Clap your hands, flick the lights, or use a wooden train whistle or other unusual sound-maker that won't be mistaken in the midst of discussion. Practice the signal several times until kids recognize it and respond to it.

Parts are all easy to follow since there are no lines to read or memorize. You'll hear what you're supposed to do as I play the CD, and do the appropriate actions. Let's get going!

Choose four children to be Jesus, the donkey, Jill Waters, and Ben Scott. Have the rest of the children form three groups: the Hosanna Crowd, the Angry Crowd, and the Crowd at Jesus' Feet. Let children put on costumes if they like.

Give Jill Waters and Ben Scott toy microphones or something to represent microphones (such as hairbrushes). Children in the Hosanna Crowd will need paper palm leaves and scarves or towels.

Explain that the stage will be divided into three areas—center stage, stage right, and stage left. Jill will be center stage. Jesus, the donkey, and the Hosanna Crowd will stand at stage right. (Jesus will move to stage left during the crucifixion scene.) Ben and the Angry Crowd will stand at stage left. The Crowd at Jesus' Feet will stand near stage left.

If you like, videotape one or two episodes of the drama. Kids won't have time to watch themselves enact the whole drama during this Venture Center, but you may have time to show them one episode before they return to The Depot.

Play "A Most Amazing Week: Part 1" (track 6). Stop the CD after this episode ends, and have the children sit down.

SAY **Great job! Wow, we covered a lot of information in that drama. This real event is recorded in each of the Gospels—things written by Matthew, Mark, Luke, and John. Tell your BibleVenture Buddies what you remember from our drama.**

Ask teams to circle up and for each child to find a partner. Ask for pairs to recount together what happened in the drama. Then have pairs discuss the following questions:

It's not essential that boys play male roles and girls play female roles. Remind kids that in drama everything is pretend. Even though they're re-enacting events from history, it's OK to have fun with the roles.

● **How do you think Jesus felt when he heard people shouting for his death?**

● **How did Jesus feel about the crowds in this story—the ones who cheered and praised him *and* the ones who were mean to him? Why?**

● **In this story, how did Jesus show that** (BP) **God loves us?**

Before asking the next question, have two or three pairs share their answers with the entire group.

SAY **Even when people were angry at or mean to Jesus, he never stopped loving them. Jesus' forgiveness and his death showed that** (BP) **God loves us. He loved us enough to give Jesus—his own precious son—to take away our sins. Now let's see what else happened.**

For the next episode, you'll need to choose nine children to play Jill Waters,

Mary Magdalene, the Stone, Peter, John, Ben Scott, two Angels, and Jesus. Have the children put on Bible-times costumes if they wish. The Stone might want to hold up a white or gray towel.

Direct Jill to stand just to the right of center stage, with a microphone. Ben should stand to the left of center stage. The Stone should stand at center stage. Other actors will enter and stand center stage as their roles are called upon.

Play "A Most Amazing Week: Part 2" (track 7) on the CD. When the track ends, stop the CD and have the actors take a bow before sitting down.

SAY **Amazing! What an incredible week! In your Venture Teams, talk about what it might have been like.**

Have Venture Teams form knee-to-knee circles and talk about the following questions.

ASK ● **Imagine you're one of Jesus' closest friends. How would you describe what happened in this story?**

● **Why was God's power important in this story?**

● **When do you see God's power in everyday life?**

● **How do you see God's *love* in everyday life?**

SAY **God's love for you was so incredible, that Jesus came back alive—to show that he's more powerful than death. God didn't want anything to stand between you and him! That's amazing news!**

Our Venture Verse says, "Dear friends, since God so loved us, we also ought to love one another" (1 John 4:11). Let's think of ways we can share that incredible love with others.

Distribute the "Breaking News!" handouts along with crayons or markers. Direct kids to draw the "front page" photo of a way they could demonstrate God's love to a friend, teacher, parent, neighbor, or sibling. Encourage kids to offer specific examples, such as "Letting my little brother have the biggest piece of cake," or "Helping my teacher clean the classroom."

When kids have finished, collect the crayons and put them away. Explain that you have one more drama. Choose a child to be the Announcer and five children to ham it up as The Stones Rolling band. The rest of the kids will be the enthusiastic audience. You may want to provide silly "rock band" costumes or instruments for The Stones Rolling.

Play "The Stones Rolling" (track 8) on the CD. When the track ends, turn off the CD and give a big round of applause for everyone.

Make life easy for your BibleVenture Buddies and yourself by making a copy of the questions for each leader. Then you won't have to keep interrupting the discussion flow to ask the next question.

SAY **Jesus *is* alive today! We can celebrate God's love and power every day by telling people that (BP) God loves us. Before we go, find ten people and shake each person's hand. Say, "God loves you, [person's name]." Then we'll make a big circle to close in prayer.**

Participate in the activity, then join the circle and pray, thanking God for Jesus' love and sacrifice. Ask God to help kids share God's love with everyone they meet each and every day.

When you close, it should be about time to move back to The Depot. Help BibleVenture Buddies escort the children back to The Depot for the closing.

If you still have time...

If you finish before it's time to head back to The Depot, use this activity.

SAY **The story of Jesus' death and resurrection is filled with emotions—sadness, pain, joy, and surprise. In your Venture Teams, work to create a silent drama. Assign parts and act out Jesus' death and resurrection without using words—only your face and body to express the emotions that people went through in this amazing, true story.**

Let groups work for about five minutes, then take turns presenting their silent dramas.

Breaking News!

Kids display God's love in new and exciting ways! Our community will never be the same.

Everytown, Everywhere

In an effort to share God's love with others, kids in your town are doing amazing acts of love and kindness. You may see kids washing dishes, giving hugs, offering to help, and even letting others go first in line. "God loves us so much...I'm just trying to pass along a little bit of that love," remarked one participant, who wouldn't give his name. "We're not doing this so people will think we're neat or anything. It's just to show God's love." *(Story continued on page A18.)*

These are provided for your reference. They're on the CD; you don't need to reproduce them.

A Most Amazing Week: Part 1

Announcer

We now interrupt this program with late-breaking news.

Jill Waters

Good evening. I'm Jill Waters with the latest news update. Jesus is dead. I repeat, Jesus is dead. This is an unexpected turn of events.

If you'll recall, just days ago there were festivities in the street celebrating Jesus. Look at this footage shot earlier this week. On your screen you see Jesus, riding on a donkey through the streets of Jerusalem. Notice that the crowds are waving their hands. Some people are spreading their cloaks on the ground so the donkey can walk on them. We'll turn up the sound and you can hear that the crowds are shouting, "Hosanna!" and "Blessed is the king who comes in the name of the Lord!"

It was quite a parade. Quite a celebration.

But the celebration has ended. Look at your screens, and you'll see footage shot earlier today. Jesus is standing in front of a crowd of men. The crowd is pointing at Jesus. Their faces are mean. They're accusing Jesus. They want him punished. A leader named Pilate cannot find Jesus guilty of any crime, so Jesus has been sent to the ruler, Herod. These men are mocking Jesus. They're beating him. They're shouting, "Crucify him!" Listen to their angry shouts.

They want Jesus killed. And that brings us up to date. Jesus *has* been crucified. Let's go to Ben Scott who's live on the scene. Ben?

Ben Scott

I'm here, Jill. As you can see, Jesus has been crucified. See him there with his arms spread? He has been nailed to a cross. His hands and feet have been nailed, and Jesus has been left there to die. And as you can see, his head is hanging down, and he's perfectly still. Jesus is dead.

The crowds are gathered around his feet and are looking up at him. Some are hateful. They're pointing their fingers and cruelly laughing at him. Some are sad. They're putting their faces into their hands and crying.

Jill, just before Jesus died, he spoke the most amazing words. He said, "Father, forgive them, for they do not know what they are doing." Even during his painful death, Jesus was thinking of others. He was taking the punishment for the wrong things the rest of us have done. Jesus gave his life as a gift. Truly amazing.

Back to you, Jill.

Jill

Thank you, Ben. Yes, it's sad news we bring. Jesus has died, giving his life for us. What a gift.

Announcer

That's our update for now. We'll keep you posted with new developments. And now back to your regularly scheduled program.

A Most Amazing Week: Part 2

Announcer

We now interrupt this program with late-breaking news.

Jill Waters

Good evening! This is Jill Waters with an update. Our last newscast had the terrible news that Jesus was dead—but we've recently discovered that *Jesus is alive*! Turn to your screen now, and you'll see our taped broadcast of what's happened in the past few minutes.

You can see Mary Magdalene walking toward the tomb of Jesus. He had been put into a cave carved in the hillside and a huge, gigantic, heavy stone had been rolled in front of the opening. Mary is walking closer to the tomb and realizes that the stone has been rolled away! See the look of surprise on her face? And then Mary sees that Jesus' body is *gone*! Gone! She's looking around frantically, but the body *is not there*!

So Mary quickly runs over to Peter and John. She waves her hands excitedly and explains that the body of Jesus is gone. Peter and John run back to the tomb with Mary.

They go inside the tomb. It's still empty!

Peter and John walk away, going home. Mary sits down and covers her face. None of them understand what has happened. They think Jesus' body has been stolen or moved.

Now let's go to Ben Scott who's there with the live report. Ben?

Ben

I'm here, Jill. Our cameras are watching Mary as she's crying beside the tomb. She stands up and sees two angels in white sitting inside the tomb. They ask her why she's crying. Mary tells them that she doesn't know where the body of Jesus is. And then Mary turns away from the angels.

A man walks up in front of her. It's Jesus, but Mary doesn't recognize him—maybe because she still has tears in her eyes. In fact, she thinks he's the gardener! But as he speaks to her, Mary realizes *it's Jesus*! *He's alive*!

Mary jumps up and down with joy! Jesus points and tells Mary to go and tell the others that he's alive.

Mary runs off to tell the others, and Jesus smiles. This has been such an *amazing* week, Jill!

Now back to you.

Jill

Thanks, Ben. It really has been an amazing week. Jesus died, but now he's alive! Jesus is powerful—so powerful that he can beat death!

Announcer

That's our update for now. And now back to your regularly scheduled program.

The Stones Rolling

Announcer

Helloooo! Welcome to the first appearance of the world's newest rock band, The Stones Rolling! Tonight we'll be hearing their debut song "The Stone Was Rolled Away."

Audience, every time you hear the band sing the line, "The stone, it was rolled away," you respond by shouting, "Jesus is alive today!"

Now put your hands together and welcome The Stones Rolling!

(Lead singer only)
Three women a-walkin',
And they were a-talkin'.
They were very, very sad
And felt very, very bad
'Cause Jesus had died on the cross.

(Band)
The stone, it was rolled away.

(Band and audience)
Jesus is alive today!

(Lead singer only)
Mary Magdalene
Had traveled with the team.
She had listened so well
To stories Jesus had to tell.

(Band)
The stone, it was rolled away.

(Band and audience)
Jesus is alive today!

(Lead singer only)
Another Mary and Salome
Had brought the spice.
To anoint Jesus' body
Would be so nice.

(Band)
The stone, it was rolled away.

(Band and audience)
Jesus is alive today!

(Lead singer only)
As they walked, I heard them say,
"Who will roll the stone away?"
It was a great big rock,
And the entrance it did block.

(Band)
The stone, it was rolled away.

(Band and audience)
Jesus is alive today!

(Lead singer only)
They saw a young man, dressed in
    white,

And these three women got quite a fright.
"Do not be afraid," the young man said,
"Jesus has risen from the dead."

(Band)
The stone, it was rolled away.

(Band and audience)
Jesus is alive today!

(Lead singer only)
"Jesus is risen!
He is not here!
Now go tell the others,
And have no fear!"

(Band)
The stone, it was rolled away.

(Band and audience)
Jesus is alive today!

(Lead singer only)
The women turned and fled.
I think Mary was ahead.
They were very afraid
Of the discovery they had made.

(Band)
The stone, it was rolled away.

(Band and audience)
Jesus is alive today!

(Band)
The stone, it was rolled away.

(Band and audience)
Jesus is alive today!

Announcer
What a show! Band, take a bow. And it's true! Jesus is alive!

Song Lyrics

I've Found Me a Treasure

(Chorus)

I've found me a treasure.

I've found a friend.

I've found Jesus and his love will never
end.

I've found me a treasure.

I've found a friend.

I've found Jesus and his love will never
end.

Jesus taught us how to love

In hopes that we may see:

No one's greater than the next;

Then he washed his disciples' feet.

(Repeat chorus)

For God he so loved the world

That he gave his only son.

That we may have eternal life

We are the chosen ones.

(Chorus)

Into My Heart

Into my heart,

Into my heart,

Come into my heart,

Lord Jesus.

Come in today.

Come in to stay.

Come into my heart,

Lord Jesus.

My God Is

My God is the God of creation.

My God made the land and the sea.

My God gave me hope and salvation.

Oh, that's what my God is to me.

(Chorus)

Father, Savior

Oh that's what my God is to me, to me!

Creator, Master

Oh that's what my God is to me.

My God is a friend to the lonely.

My God sets the prisoner free.

My God is a loving companion.

Oh that's what my God is to me.

(Chorus)

Christ Arose

Low in the grave he lay,

Jesus, my Savior.

Waiting the coming day,

Jesus, my Lord.

Up from the grave he arose!

With a mighty triumph o'er his foes.

He arose a victor from the dark domain.

And he lives forever with his saints to reign.

He arose!

He arose!

Hallelujah, Christ arose!

(Repeat all)

Jesus Is All the World to Me

Jesus is all the world to me.

My life, my joy, my all.

He is my strength

From day to day.

Without him I would fall.

When I am sad, to him I go

No other one can cheer me so.

When I am sad, he makes me glad.

He's my friend.

(Repeat)

Job Description: BibleVenture Buddy

BibleVenture Buddies have the joy—and the challenge—of connecting with kids in a deep, significant way.

As a BibleVenture Buddy, here's what you'll become to the kids in your care...

A trusted friend. You're a grown-up who's glad these kids came, who knows their names, who's been praying about what's important to them. Your focused attention and listening ear help your kids realize they're important to you—and to God.

A role model. How you interact with kids sets the tone for how they'll interact with each other.

A guide. Instead of being the "teacher" with all the answers, you're someone who asks great questions. You jump in and enthusiastically do the activities *they* do at BibleVenture. You gently guide kids as they discover how to apply God's Word to their lives and enter into a deeper relationship with Jesus.

A steady influence in kids' lives. From week to week, you're there with a smile and kind word. You don't demand that kids perform to earn your approval. You don't give kids grades. You're in their corner, dependably cheering them on.

And as you serve God and the kids in your Venture Team, you'll help Jesus touch kids' hearts and change their lives—forever.

To be a spectacularly successful BibleVenture Buddy, it helps if you...
- love God,
- enjoy being with children,
- can be reflective and thoughtful,
- are comfortable talking with children about Jesus,
- believe children can understand and live God's Word,
- are accepting and supportive of children,
- model God's love in what you say and do, and
- like to laugh and have fun.

Responsibilities

As a BibleVenture Buddy, your responsibilities include...
- attending any scheduled training sessions,
- greeting children as they arrive,
- accompanying your Venture Team when traveling to a Center,
- joining in activities with your Venture Team,
- encouraging the kids in your Venture Team,
- facilitating discussions with your Venture Team,
- actively seeking to grow spiritually and in your leadership skills,
- assisting Center Leaders as needed,
- overseeing the sign-out sheet for your Venture Team, and
- praying for the children you serve.

Job Description: BibleVenture Center Leader

BibleVenture Center Leaders provide fun, engaging experiences for small groups of kids. Because the focus of each Center is slightly different, the skills required to lead each Center change from Center to Center, too.

But there are a few things *every* effective and successful Center Leader has in common. Successful Center Leader...

- love God,
- enjoy and value children,
- are energetic and upbeat,
- maintain a positive attitude,
- can organize and motivate children to listen,
- are humble,
- are observant,
- attend scheduled leader training,
- prepare lessons thoroughly and with excellence, and
- model God's love in what they say and do.

At the BibleVenture Center program, Leaders serve in these two areas:

1. The Depot

The Depot Leader is the "up front" leader, helping kids transition into BibleVenture by leading a brief, fun, upbeat program.

You're responsible for...

- collecting necessary supplies,
- preparing and leading the weekly openings and closings with excellence,
- reinforcing the daily Bible Point as you lead,
- leading music, or finding someone to help you do so, and
- praying for the children and BibleVenture Buddies you serve.

2. Venture Centers

Center Leaders encourage kids to form a lasting relationship with their BibleVenture Buddies, team members, and Jesus by leading an excellent forty-minute lesson.

You're responsible for...

- collecting necessary supplies,
- preparing and leading the weekly program with excellence,
- reinforcing the daily Bible Point as you lead,
- asking questions that will be discussed among the small groups (not with you!),
- cleaning up your area after your lesson, and
- praying for the children and volunteers in your BibleVenture program.

Job Description: BibleVenture Servant Leader

BibleVenture Servant Leaders support the BibleVenture program by jumping in to help where needed. You have a few assigned tasks but will probably do far more as you're asked to substitute for a missing BibleVenture Buddy, or help out with a drama, or gather supplies, or...

Successful BibleVenture Servant Leaders...

- love God,
- enjoy and value children,
- are energetic and upbeat,
- maintain a positive attitude,
- are humble,
- are observant,
- attend scheduled leader training,
- have servant hearts, and
- model God's love in what they say and do.

Responsibilities

As a BibleVenture Servant Leader, your responsibilities include...

- attending any scheduled training sessions,
- greeting children as they arrive,
- staffing the Depot ticket window during the opening and closing times,
- encouraging kids and leaders,
- actively seeking to grow spiritually and in your leadership skills,
- assisting Center Leaders as needed, and
- praying for the children and leaders in your BibleVenture program.

BibleVenture Sign-In and Sign-Out Sheet

We value the children trusted to our care! Please sign your child in and out. And if there are people who are not permitted to pick up your child, please provide that information to our staff.

CHILD'S NAME:	PERSON SIGNING CHILD IN:	PERSON SIGNING CHILD OUT:	Check if ONLY the person signing child in can sign child out.

Bonus Training Session!

In the kingdom of God, everything starts with a relationship.

A growing relationship with God *is* the goal of a children's ministry, and any program that helps kids connect with Jesus, each other, and caring adult leaders is a successful program—no matter how large or small the program might be.

This one-hour session will help you encourage leaders to highly value building relationships with children.

How to Be Wildly Successful at Encouraging Relationship Building

At the end of this workshop, participants will be able to

● work together to determine how friendships can form in your BibleVenture program,

● clearly explain how they can practically help children form a friendship with Jesus, and

● take steps to form or strengthen friendships among themselves as BibleVenture Leaders.

Supplies

● Bible

● name tags

● markers

● items that need each other to function well, such as a hammer and a nail, paper and pencil, baseball and ball glove, CD player and CD, book and bookmark, and paint and paintbrush

● white board or newsprint

● 1 copy of the "Word Search" handout for each participant

● transparency paper

● overhead projector

● snacks

Before the Workshop

Set up a table at the front of the room. Scatter the items on the table so the complementary items aren't near each other.

Draw two lines that divide your white board or piece of newsprint into three columns. At the top of the left column, write "Life." At the top of the middle column, write "BibleVenture." At the top of the right column, write "Jesus."

Make a photocopy onto a transparency of the "Word Search" from page 92. Set up an overhead projector with the transparency.

Before participants begin arriving, ask God to encourage your BibleVenture Leaders through you, and that you'll all use what you learn to help kids grow closer to Jesus. Ask God to bless your leaders as they minister to children and other adult leaders.

Greet participants warmly as they arrive. Ask each person to fill out a name tag with his or her first name in capital letters.

After participants have gathered, ask them to be seated.

SAY **Think about someone who's a close friend in your life right now—someone who's not here at our meeting. Think about when you met your friend, how you've gotten closer to that person, and what makes your relationship so special.**

When you've thought of someone, come up to this table and take any item, then return to your seat.

When each participant has an item, ask participants to find the person with the item that complements the one in their hands. For example, the person with a jar of peanut butter will need to find the person with the jar of jelly.

SAY **Tell your new partner about the friend you just thought about. Discuss how you got to know your friend, what makes your relationship tick, and why that friend is so special to you. You'll each have two minutes to share.**

When the first two minutes have passed, tell pairs to take another two minutes. Explain that this would be a good time for those who haven't shared to begin telling about their close friends.

When the final two minutes have passed, ask volunteers to share how their partners got to know their close friends and why their relationship is special.

Thank volunteers for sharing.

SAY **We all have close friends. And we develop those friendships in different ways. Here's a question for you: How many of you grew closer to your partner's friend by listening to what your partner said for two minutes?**

You will probably find a minimal number of hands rise.

SAY **Now, how many of you actually *formed* a close relationship with your**

partner's friend by listening to what your partner said? You feel you know the person well enough to call and share something deeply personal?

Fewer hands will rise!

SAY **Listening to someone tell about a friend doesn't bring us into an intimate relationship with that friend very well. We have to experience those relationships. What are some ways we build relationships with others?**

Allow volunteers to give several responses. You will likely hear things like: spending time together, experiencing challenges together, having things in common, and having fun together.

SAY **It's nice to hear about others' friendships, but it doesn't bring us into a relationship with that person. How is that like or unlike the way we may teach children about Jesus?**

Have volunteers answer.

SAY **Let's try another activity to help us grow closer to a friend.**

Distribute a folded copy of the "Word Search" handout to each person. Caution people that they shouldn't open up the papers until you tell them to do so.

SAY **Open up your handouts now. I want you to find the name of your partner's friend in this word search. You'll have thirty seconds. Go.**

At the end of the thirty seconds, tell participants to again fold their handouts.

SAY **Now how many of you are closer to your partner's best friend?**

You probably will not see any hands rise now, either.

SAY **It's certainly easy to tell about a friend, or to give someone a word search puzzle to figure out. But those approaches to Christian education aren't very helpful in promoting relationships, are they?**

At our BibleVenture program, we have unique opportunities to help children not just know *about* our friend, Jesus, but to actually get to know Jesus on a deep, intimate level. That's our goal: for children to know, love, and follow Jesus.

Today we're going to consider some ways to effectively bring children into a close relationship with Jesus. They may not remind you much of how Sunday school has been done in the past, but that's OK. Our goal at BibleVenture isn't just to give information—it's to help transformation happen as kids meet Jesus, and grow in their friendship with Jesus.

And friendship is something Jesus wants with us.

Open your Bible and read aloud John 15:15.

SAY **That's our goal. We don't want children to just know about Jesus, or to respect Jesus, or even admire him from afar. We want to encourage children to be in a *relationship* with Jesus—one where Jesus would call them his friends.**

So how can we make that happen?

Let's find out.

The items you have in your pairs relate to one another in a unique way. We'll use your items as we discover how to be relational in our ministry.

Before we let you use your jelly jars and hammers, let's take a look at what *relational* means in different aspect of our lives. Then we'll connect it to ministry. With your partner, brainstorm things in our lives that help build relationships—especially relationships we'd describe as "friendships." Think of activities, conversations, words, gestures, and anything else that would help a friendship to grow. I'll give you five minutes to come up with as many ideas as you can.

Give pairs about four and a half minutes, then give a thirty-second warning. When five minutes are up, call time and ask for volunteers to share several ways friendships are developed in our lives.

Affirm each suggestion, and probe any suggestions you don't understand with open-ended questions like, "Tell me more about that" or "Help me understand what you mean—what's an example?"

Write each response under the "Life" column on the board. Make sure you write each suggestion legibly and large enough for everyone to see.

One quick way to move through the suggestions is to ask one pair to share their ideas, then for each subsequent pair to contribute any ideas that aren't already covered on the board.

SAY **These are great ways to build friendships! Now spend five more minutes with your partner to brainstorm what these may look like in our BibleVenture program. How can you promote friendships here in our program, based on our life list?**

For example, maybe we identified "spending quality time one-on-one" as a way friendships grow.

Here at our BibleVenture program, our BibleVenture Buddies have an opportunity to do that with children who arrive early. Buddies can ask kids

how they're doing, and actively listen to what kids say. Discuss how other friendship-building ideas translate from our day-to-day lives to our ministry here.

Give pairs four and a half minutes, then give a thirty-second warning. When five minutes are up, call time and ask for volunteers to share several ways relationships are developed in our ministries.

Affirm each suggestion, and probe any suggestions you don't understand with open-ended questions such as "Tell me more about that" or "Help me understand what you mean—what might that look like?"

Write each response under the "Ministry" column on the board. Make sure you write each suggestion legibly and large enough for everyone to see.

SAY **We've discovered how friendships form in real life—person to person. And we've discovered how those friendship-forming techniques can translate to our BibleVenture ministry here at church.**

But is this how a friendship with Jesus forms, too? Is this how kids get to know Jesus and enter into a friendship with him? Remember, young children are concrete thinkers; it's tough for them to form relationships with people they don't see in person. And if _that's_ tough, forming a relationship with Jesus can be even tougher.

Yet, that's our goal: for kids to form a relationship with Jesus.

So how does it happen?

For instance, we know that spending time one-on-one is healthy for forming relationships. And we see our Buddies have the opportunity to do that. How can that help kids form a relationship with Jesus?

For young children, the answer might be that we talk about our relationship with Jesus. We make sure we're transparent about having a friendship with Jesus, and we live our lives in a way that reflects that friendship.

For older children in our program, we might probe about the relationship they have—or don't have—with Jesus. We can dig deeper.

Ask partners to form foursomes and then work their way down the columns to see how kids might form a friendship with Jesus through your ministry, valuing and implementing friendship-building actions.

Please note: This might sound like a simple conversation, but it's a difficult one. That's because this requires a great deal of thought, and because some of your volunteers might envision a friendship with Jesus forming primarily through knowledge. That is, knowing the books of the Bible or key Bible verses might be the most important way to get to know Jesus.

For some people, mastering information *is* a critical friendship component... but that's not true for everyone.

And it's especially not true for children.

Think about watching children play together on a playground or at a camp. How many life details do children require before deciding to enter into a relationship with another child? Very few. Children want to know they're safe and that the other person is caring. After that, the details generally get filled in through experience that happens within the relationship.

The point: Jesus is trustworthy. Jesus is caring. It's OK for children to enter into a friendship with him without mastering all the related facts that will come later.

If we insist on the facts coming first, we're putting up an obstacle that doesn't exist for children...and isn't required by Christ.

Is that something we really want to do?

Be sensitive to the paradigm shift this "friendship value" may place on some of your teachers who are now serving as BibleVenture Buddies. Rather than sharing information with children, these teachers are now facilitating discovery. Instead of giving instructions, they're entering into activities with children. It may be an entirely new world. Instead of "teaching a class," they're "building friendships with John and Ric and Rachel and Kelli."

Give foursomes four and a half minutes to talk, then give a thirty-second warning. When five minutes are up, call time and ask for volunteers to share several ways relationships are developed in our ministries.

Affirm each suggestion, and probe any suggestions you don't understand with open-ended questions like, "Tell me more about that" or "Help me understand what you mean—what might that look like?"

Take time to move from principles into specifics; as you do so, you're developing new elements of your volunteers' job descriptions.

When you've got the third column filled out, step back and read it aloud.

SAY **Wow—it took some work to get to this list, but what a list it is! These are the things we can integrate into our BibleVenture program that will help children develop a friendship with Jesus. Is there anything more important we could be doing?**

Wrap up by assuring your volunteers that you'll send a list of the three columns to each of them (and follow up promptly to do so!). Then ask for volunteers to share what insights came to them through this session. You might hear things like, "I didn't realize how important my relating to the kids is," or "I can see now why it's important to get to the church fifteen minutes early so I can greet children."

Thank your volunteers for their commitment to God and to the children your church serves. Remind them that they're planting seeds in young lives that God will bless, and that the harvest will be a hundredfold.

Ask foursomes to stand together and hold hands and to close in prayer, asking God's blessings on your church's BibleVenture program and your relationships on your teaching team.

Finally, point to the snacks and remind participants that you left time for talking intentionally—it's important that leaders develop friendships too!

Word Search

```
E    S    K    P    A    R    L
K    E    P    L    O    K    P
A    M    N    T    H    O    M
T    I    P    B    I    G    F
M    A    B    L    E    C    W
R    I    C    F    N    O    P
G    U    S    H    L    I    D
B    L    A    T    Y    H    E
Q    H    L    V    I    C    K
J    A    M    P    L    O    Y
I    H    Z    E    G    Y    O
S    N    E    W    P    V    B
U    L    O    P    F    C    M
```

Jesus—Death Destroyer

BibleVenture Invitation Letter

Dear Kate,

A spectacular parade, midnight arrest and trial, a brutal murder, and the mysterious disappearance of a body...

Sounds like a Hollywood movie, doesn't it?

Except this isn't a movie...it's true! And you can learn all about it!

You're invited to join us at *BibleVenture Centers™: Jesus—Death Destroyer* each Sunday night starting July 6 at 6.

We'll meet for four Sundays in a row—all July—and you won't want to miss a single night!

Each one-hour program will have you visiting a different BibleVenture Center. One week you may be acting in a fun, no-lines-to-learn drama presentation. Another week you may be crafting an art project to take home. There's always something different, and it's always fun!

Tell your mom or dad right now that you want to join your friends at BibleVenture on July 6! Circle the date on the family calendar! That's the date the adventure begins...and who knows where it will end?

It just might change your life!

Sincerely,
Audrey Ferris
BibleVenture Director,
First Church
555-1212

Invite kids to your BibleVenture Centers™: Jesus—Death Destroyer *program! Adapt this invitation to fit your schedule and church letterhead, then send a copy to each child in your Sunday school. Post copies on community bulletin boards, and send invitations to neighborhood children who visited your vacation Bible school, too!*

Leader Encouragement Pages

Can you imagine doing a BibleVenture program without volunteer leaders? It wouldn't happen!

So thank your leaders weekly with these four reproducible pages. You have one page for each week of this BibleVenture program.

Each week, make a copy of one page for each of your leaders. Slip copies into envelopes, and send each volunteer an encouraging letter. Make it even more special by jotting a personal note on each copy you send.

The volunteer experts at Group's Church Volunteer Central (www.churchvolunteercentral.com) report that a leading reason volunteers resign their positions is that volunteers don't feel recognized and appreciated.

You can help your precious children's ministry leaders feel valued by saying "Thanks!" on a regular basis...and these pages will help!

"Then God will strengthen you with his own great power. And you will not give up when troubles come, but you will be patient."

—Colossians 1:11 (International Children's Bible)

What troubles you today?
Ask God for strength—and share your struggle with a team member who can pray for you!

"You will receive your salvation with joy as you would draw water from a well. At that time you will say, 'Praise the Lord and worship him. Tell everyone what he has done and how great he is.'"

—Isaiah 12:3-4 (New Century Version)

When you're serving kids in our BibleVenture, you're doing what Isaiah prophesied. What a privilege!

"So let's not allow ourselves to get fatigued doing good. At the right time we will harvest a good crop if we don't give up, or quit."

—*Galatians 6:9 (The Message)*

You're planting good seed in young hearts. The harvest will come in time. Don't grow tired of being a Christlike influence in the lives of children!

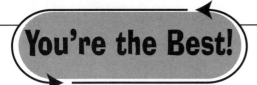

You're the Best!

"Be devoted to one another in brotherly love. Honor one another above yourselves."

—Romans 12:10

We're a team! At our next BibleVenture, give another children's worker a hug, a handshake, or a high five!

How to Connect With Kids

Dear BibleVenture Leader,

For just a moment, think about your favorite teacher in grade school.

Can you remember that person? Picture the teacher's face and—if you can—the classroom where you spent time with that teacher. Fix that face and space in your mind.

Now think about *why* that teacher was your favorite.

I'm willing to bet it wasn't because the teacher was especially good at providing instruction about geography or at teaching the alphabet. While your favorite teacher might have sparkled at his or her teaching skills, it's not likely that's why you connected in such a meaningful way.

Rather, I'm willing to bet that you connected with that teacher *personally*. You had a *relationship* with him or her, and it's that relationship you remember so warmly.

Here's what you probably *don't* remember: Your favorite teacher probably did lots of little things to connect with you, to communicate warmth and caring. Maybe it was tucking a Valentine's Day card in your box or remembering your birthday. Maybe it was simply knowing your name when so many adults didn't bother to learn it.

Whatever those little things were, it's likely that no matter how special they made you feel, the teacher did the same things with other students, too.

That's right: *Your* favorite teacher is probably other peoples' favorite teacher! The little habits and connection skills used with you probably endeared your teacher to other kids, too.

It's the little things that count—and connect.

Now think about your role in our BibleVenture program. You have contact with kids week after week, and that means you have the potential to be the teacher someone remembers fondly twenty years from now when picturing a face from the past.

That's right—*you* can be that children's leader who has such a huge impact on a child that you're remembered long after the child has become an adult.

To do that you'll need to do your job well at BibleVenture, but you'll need to do something more.

You'll need to connect with kids.

I want to suggest three "little things" that will go a long way toward connecting you with kids. They're habits you can easily develop, and they'll cost you nothing...but they'll give kids a bridge into a relationship with you.

How to Connect With Kids

1. Be approachable.

Ever talk with someone standing on a stepladder or on steps? Uncomfortable, isn't it?

That's what it's like for children to talk with adults, especially tall ones. Kids crane their necks and strain to hear what grown-ups are saying. And then there's the "other challenge": what to call you.

Here are some easy ways to be approachable to children...

• **Kneel when you're talking with kids.** This removes the obstacle of your height difference and lets you engage children in eye-to-eye conversation.

• **Be cheerful—and smile.** When adults appear grumpy or angry, children often wonder if it's their fault. So be deliberate about leaving your disgust with the crack in your car windshield out in the parking lot with your car. When you enter the room for BibleVenture, be smiling and welcoming.

• **Wear a name tag.** This not only helps children remember your name but also signals how you want to be addressed. If you write, "Mrs. Smith," that's what kids will call you. But if you write, "Sally," that gives children permission to call you by your first name.

• **Use children's name in conversations.** If your memory is wired so names escape you, go to the trouble of having kids wear name tags. Or simply make it important enough to learn names.

• **Wear comfortable clothing that lets you enter into activities.** In any given BibleVenture program, your kids might be painting, skipping, or pretending they're in an earthquake as they roll around on the floor. Be dressed so you can join them!

2. Share your life—within reason.

Grown-ups lead lives that are completely different from lives lived by children. It's like we're on different planets. That's why it's critical that, in a healthy way, you share what's happening in your life.

Because kids aren't your peers, you need to be careful about what you share. Never make a child uncomfortable or responsible for more information than he or she can bear.

That still leaves plenty of material that's appropriate to discuss—your family, for instance, or upcoming travel plans. General health issues might be appropriate, too, and work- or school-related topics.

Here are several simple ways to share your life with your children...

• **When it's prayer time, share something.** Asking children to pray for you and your life communicates that you value both prayer and your kids.

How to Connect With Kids

• *Bring in a picture of your family to pass around.* Maybe it's your husband and kids, your parents, or even a candid picture of your dog (do they take formal dog photos?). It doesn't matter what the photo is; the fact that you're passing it around gives children a sense that you live in the real world. You're not just the person they see at church.

3. Have fun.

The children's version of that famous saying reads this way: "The families that play together, stay together."

At our BibleVenture we're trying to build a family atmosphere. That's why children are in small groups with consistent adult leadership. That's why we encourage relationship-building.

And what do they call the person in a family who never enters into games or parties? A *party pooper*, that's what!

Don't be a party pooper. Dive into activities with your kids as your playmates. Your participation gives you a shared experience with the kids and provides a richer, more authentic debriefing time after visiting Venture Centers.

Here are some ways to have fun with children...

• *Check your dignity at the door.* OK, maybe you don't particularly want to stick your hands in paint and leave a handprint on a banner. So what? Do it anyway, and enter into the spirit of the moment alongside your kids. Sing along even if you don't sing well. Play the game even if you know you won't win. Play a part in the drama even if you know there's no Academy Award in your future.

• *Participate in everything.* That means the snack, the skits, the games...everything. If you give yourself permission to opt out of some activities, your kids will do the same. Your participation sets the standard—make sure that standard is "we do it all." If you're not participating, there's no chance for you to have fun with your kids!

• *Don't be competitive.* If you feel you should make a good showing because you're the grown-up, get over it. Relax and enjoy yourself, and consider it all joy should a child beat you across the finish line in the toe-to-heel relay.

After all, is winning that race really so important for your career advancement? A high score for you means nothing; to a child it's what makes a great day.

How to Connect With Kids

How hard is it to connect with kids in a significant, life-changing way?

It takes a decision that kids are important, and your volunteering to serve at BibleVenture shows you've already decided that.

It takes a childlike (not *childish*) heart and a willingness to let others in.

And it takes placing good connection habits into your daily life and ministry. You can start with those identified above, but they're just the tip of the iceberg. Watch adults who kids love, and you'll find more and more behaviors that tear down barriers and build bridges instead. Plug those behaviors into our own ministry style; you'll see kids warm up to you even more.

God bless you as you serve kids. You're doing work that will change lives—the lives of your kids and your own life, too!

Make a copy of this letter for each of your BibleVenture volunteers!

Tips From the Trenches for
BibleVenture Buddies

"I have a child who absolutely refuses to write or draw in his visa. And when I insist, he doodles and draws tanks. What do I do?"

Be aware that there are children who dislike writing and drawing, and nothing you say or do will change that.

Visas are a tool for helping kids remember the lessons and reinforce the Bible truth. If a child won't use the visa, try to accomplish those purposes without it. Pair up with this child and talk through the questions in the visa. Help this child see value in the process by engaging in it yourself.

And at bare minimum, you *can* insist that kids who choose to not participate don't distract others.

"Hey, what if I want to tell kids more about the Bible—to show them verses that will help them grow spiritually? Can I do that?"

Of course. There are times it's absolutely appropriate for you to speak God's truth into a situation. But think of how you feel when you're talking with a friend about something you're thinking through and your friend suddenly starts handing out advice. How does that feel?

Kids get that *all* the time—especially from adults. What they *most* need to do is grow in their relationship with God, so keep focused on that.

Plus, BibleVenture Centers deliberately seeks to take a simple Bible truth and plant it deep in kids' hearts and minds. That doesn't happen instantly. If it takes a few weeks and the kids truly grasp the significance of a Bible truth, it's worth the time investment.

You can clutter the process if you insist on dealing with a dozen Scripture passages lightly rather than one in depth.

Sometimes less is truly more.

"We use BibleVenture Centers during a midweek slot. Some of my leaders bring their own kids, and some parents drop off their kids a half hour before we get started. What do I do with those kids while we're waiting to get going?"

You can't overestimate the value of a special box full of easy-to-play group games like beanbags, Tick-Tack-Toe, and ball toss. Kids who arrive early take their pick of these games as music plays in the background. A few minutes before the opening Depot program, put the games away.

BibleVenture Buddies can join in the games, or just let the kids play together.

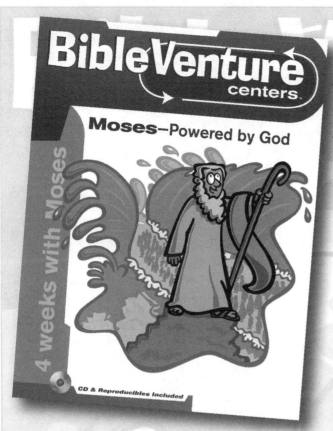

Moses—Powered by God

4 weeks with Moses

CD & Reproducibles Included

Your kids will explore how God used Moses, and discover how God can use them, too...at *Moses—Powered by God!*

"Cast your cares on the Lord and he will sustain you" *(Psalm 55:22).*

At *Moses—Powered by God!* kids visit four Venture Centers...

● *The Music Center* where kids explore instruments, discover how to make sounds that remind them of Moses' life, and along the way they learn God used Moses...and God can use them, too!

● *The Arts & Crafts Center* where they'll discover the early years of Moses as they craft Baby Moses figures and floating baskets.

● *The Drama Center* where they'll explore the life of Moses and discover that just like God used Moses, God can use them, too!

● *The Games Center* where kids will play games that teach them all about the plagues visited on the Egyptians.

At **BibleVenture** your children won't just learn God's Word...they'll *experience* it!

Order today at www.group.com or call 1-800-747-6060 ext.1370

enjoy even more Rotational, Learning-Center fun!

Choose from two VBS Programs this year!

Take your pick of Group's easy Vacation Bible School program, or the new environmental VBS where you turn your church into a first-century Bibleland village!

Both VBS programs feature small groups of children rotating between learning centers, just like at BibleVenture. And also like at BibleVenture, kids form friendships with other children, adult leaders, and with Jesus!

Make VBS Fun and Relational!

Find out this year's easy-to-decorate VBS theme!
Visit your local Christian bookstore or call
1-800-635-0404
today!

Like the fun and efficiency of having small groups of children rotate between teaching stations?

Then you'll love these resources! They each use the same learning-center model, make it easy to recruit volunteers, and give you loads of teaching options!

Option #1

GROUP'S easy VBS!

It's all here—an exciting theme; cool decorating ideas; and learning centers where kids sing, play, craft neat stuff, snack, and experience Bible stories in ways they'll remember forever.

Plus, kids receive daily challenges that help them apply what they learn!

Option #2

GROUP'S Bible-Times VBS!

Your kids will step back in time as they experience Jesus' teaching in the context of a first-century culture. Kids enjoy new traditions, foods, arts and crafts projects...and you'll see little eyes light up with understanding!